NO LONGER A
SECRET

NO LONGER A
SECRET

The church and
violence
against women

Aruna Gnanadason

BOOK SERIES

WCC Publications, Geneva

Dedicated to

Mercy, my mother

and

Joy, my mother-in-law

Two women who gave me life and taught me courage,
each in her own way.

Second revised edition 1997

Cover design: Rob Lucas
Cover picture: Rob Lucas
Cover p. 4 photo: WCC/Peter Williams

ISBN 2-8254-1098-5

© 1993 WCC Publications, World Council of Churches,
150 route de Ferney, 1211 Geneva 20, Switzerland

No. 58 in the Risk book series

Printed in The Netherlands

Table of Contents

1. Facing the Reality

> "Go back to him... learn how to adjust to his moods... don't do anything that would provoke his anger... Christ suffered and died for you on the Cross... Can't you bear some suffering too?"

This is a voice of the church — the words of a priest counselling a woman who was being battered by her husband every single day of her married life. She went to the church for refuge and for moral and spiritual support. What she received instead was advice to learn submissiveness and obedience in a distorted relationship and an abusive marriage.

The response to women's cries for justice and fair treatment is not always so heartless. There are occasions when women have experienced the caring concern of a community of Christians. There are exceptional examples of radical actions of solidarity taken by the church. But by and large, the churches around the world have remained silent about violence against women. Too often it is treated as a marginal concern, relegated to the attention of *women* in the church, not recognized as an issue central to the church's life and witness because of its deep and dehumanizing effects on the lives of women in the community.

When women live in violent contexts or in constant fear it has a deleterious effect on the development of societies as a whole. Unfortunately, this is not taken as seriously as it should be by either the church or other institutions in society. MATCH, a Canadian nongovernmental organization, concludes that:

> Violent acts against women the world over attack their dignity as human beings and leave them vulnerable and fearful. Conditioned to undervalue their skills and abilities and paralyzed by real fears of violence and retribution, women are marginalized in society and forced out of decision-making processes which shape and determine the development of their communities. [1]

Women have to be able to participate fully in their country's plans, policies and programmes if development is to take place. As long as they are stifled in their participation by fear of violence, as long as they are reluctant to take up leadership positions because they are subject to physical or emotional abuse, the progress of whole populations will suffer.

It is the denial of this truth and the church's failure to offer adequate support or a concerted response that have prompted women around the world to raise the issue of violence against them as a priority area on the agenda of the Ecumenical Decade of the Churches in Solidarity with Women (1988-1998). With alarming consistency, women from all regions of the world are identifying the various forms of violence they live with and calling on the church to respond.

Identifying the forms of violence

It should be recognized that women have begun to speak out their pain only in recent times. For centuries, violence against women has been one of the world's best kept secrets. Even today, published statistics from around the world on crimes against women do not reflect the full picture since they refer only to *reported* incidents of violence. Within the very male-dominated contexts of all societies, much violence against women goes unreported. Moreover, at every stage — from the family to the church to the police to the law courts — the understanding of "violence" excludes or ignores many forms of emotional, psychological and physical abuse that women experience.

No region or country is exempt from expressions of violence against women. Statistics collected by the New York-based International Women's Tribune Centre from women around the world are staggering, to say the least.[2]
— In Costa Rica, one of every two women can expect to be a victim of violence at some point in her life.
— In Jamaica, where rape is not a criminal offence, 1088 cases of rape and carnal abuse were reported in 1989.

— In Canada, one in four women can expect to be assaulted at some point in their lives, half of these before the age of 17.

— According to UN reports, India leads the world in "custodial" rape (rape committed by men in positions of power such as police officers, prison and hospital staff, doctors).

— In the US, a woman is beaten every 15 seconds; every six minutes a rape occurs; every day four women are killed by their batterers.

— A report by the Mexican Federation of Women's Trade Unions says that 95 percent of Mexican women workers are victims of sexual harassment in their workplaces.

— Three-quarters of the women interviewed in an International Labour Office (ILO) study of plantation workers in Sri Lanka said they had been beaten by their husbands or estate superintendents.

— In the Philippines, one out of every two women arrested by the military is forced to undress, according to a study on rape by the military. Fourteen percent reported that they were slapped, boxed or severely mauled; another 14 percent were harassed and threatened with rape or death.

— In Peru, one of every four girl children will be the victim of sexual abuse before she reaches her sixteenth birthday, and a third of all adult women report that they have been forced to have sex against their will.

Many other sources provide evidence of equally horrifying proportions. *African Woman* tells the story of eleven women who were raped by soldiers in April 1991 while they were being held with thousands of other civilians in Uganda for identity checks and questioning.[3] The picture is clear: all over the world women are being brutalized and violated.

Recent research points to an even more frightening trend: women belong to an "endangered species". On the basis of demographic statistics from around the world, Harvard economist Amartya Sen estimates that the number of females "missing" due to biases against them could well be over 100 million. One reason for this shortfall is that girls are not allowed to benefit as much as boys from improvements in health care and nutrition that are lowering death rates. Under normal circumstances, from 5 to 6 percent more boys than girls are born; and at every age thereafter males die at higher rates than females. In the US, Britain and Poland, for example, there are about 105 females to every 100 males. In India, by contrast, the 1991 census showed that there are only 92.9 females to every 100 males, down from 93.4 in 1981. The 1990 census in China found just 93.8 females to every 100 males, compared with 94.1 at the time of the 1982 census. These and similar statistics from Afghanistan, Bangladesh, Bhutan, Nepal, Pakistan, Papua New Guinea and Turkey found in the United Nations 1991 report on "The World's Women" confirm that in many countries, the ratio between women and men is decreasing.[4] This form of violence against women cannot be ignored.

The roots of the problem

It is necessary to unearth the roots of the violence to which women are exposed if we are to combat it effectively. In recent years, women have used the term "patriarchy" to articulate one understanding of existing unequal power relations in the world, and to describe the violence that women face in their homes, in the workplace and elsewhere in society. Such violence is seen as an expression of the wider violent and militarized context of the world in which we live. Patriarchy is identified as a system of "graded subjugation" in which some have power over others. This power can be manifested in economic, political, social or cultural terms.

The new definition, which goes beyond how the church has traditionally understood the term "patriarchy", underscores the fact that men in all societies have an unfair edge over women. It is true that it is not only women who live in violence but all people on the fringes of society — men, women and children, the "little ones" of this world, who live without power under the shadow of death-dealing forces. But in all contexts, women are the primary victims.

Crisis points in the world manifest the general culture of violence and militarism pervading political, economic, social and cultural life in every region. Global economic and social structures create the atmosphere for unequal power relations between and within nations. This engineers inequalities and keeps intact the atmosphere of violence of which women are special targets.

In every society, they are the most vulnerable and, along with children, the ones who bear the brunt of the world's injustice. Their sexuality is exploited, as is evident from the image of women projected in the media. Their labour is exploited, and any crisis in the economic structure hits women first. Women in the South suffer tremendous hardship working long hours in unhealthy and and unhygienic surroundings. They eke out a living in squatter settlements and slums and as the rural poor, lacking basic amenities, nutrition, health care, maternity and child care facilities. Women have always been viewed as a reserve army of cheap and docile labour. The recession and cutbacks on social welfare spending affect the lives of women in the North as well, particularly single mothers, migrants and refugee women and workers in poorly paid jobs. There is no doubt that in all our societies, women are the poorest of the poor and the most economically marginalized, unfairly burdened by the current global economic crisis.

What is even more insidious is that the violence women experience is considered to be secondary to the other forms of violence prevalent in the world. But it cannot be denied that "sexism kills". According to the well-known crusader against gender violence, Charlotte Bunch, "there is increasing documentation of the many ways in which being female is life-threatening," and a woman is unsafe at every stage of life, even before she is born.[5]

Bunch provides a number of examples to illustrate her point. *Before birth*, the medical procedure of amniocentesis continues to be used solely to determine the sex of the foetus, leading to widespread abortion of female foetuses, particularly in China and India, where more males than females are born even though natural birth ratios would produce more females. *During childhood*, the World Health Organization (WHO) reports, girls in many countries are fed less, breast-fed for shorter periods of time, taken to doctors less frequently than boys. As a result, girls are physically and mentally maimed by malnutrition or die at higher rates than boys. *In adulthood*, Bunch says, the denial of women's right to control their reproductive capacities threatens their lives, especially where it is combined with poverty and poor health services.

It is thus evident that the increased incidence of such violence against women as wife-beating, rape and dowry deaths cannot be dealt with as only crime statistics or dismissed as individual aberrations of demented males (though there are frequent examples of men who are passing through some deep psychological crisis going on a rampage of violence against women). Most incidents of violence are manifestations of social structures that perpetuate personal and systemic injustice.

Whatever its form, violence has its roots in distorted power relations. Patriarchal violence has not been adequately understood nor acknowledged as a necessary framework for analyzing structural inequalities in society. Yet unless there is a shift in the way unequal power relations are defined and a challenge to concepts that legitimize the imbalance of power in the hands of a few, who are largely males, there is no way to tackle the systemic roots of the violence against women, nor to respond adequately to individual incidents. This still remains an open challenge.

Women have attributed the increased violence of the past two decades to a "backlash" against the women's movement. There has been resistance to the organized voices of women and their determination to speak out against all that oppresses them, and serious attempts to undermine women's struggles for basic human rights. One way in which this is done is to develop a sophisticated methodology of control, including the use of force, to "teach women a lesson" so that they will know better than to rebel or question their status and position.

Violence in the lives of women may take blatant forms. Or it may be subtle. In either case, it eats into women's psyches, demoralizing them and lowering their self-esteem. To categorize the specific forms of violence women face as "overt" or "covert" is not to imply that there are some forms of violence which are "private" and therefore can be resisted in an isolated manner. All violence against women has systemic roots. The categories described below are not rigid, because they are interrelated. Nor is the list exhaustive; it is rather an attempt to identify and describe some expressions of violence.

Overt forms of violence

Violence in the domestic sphere

In the past, it was often virtually impossible to know what happened inside the family home, but since women have dared to speak out their pain, this information is no longer secret. Even so, statistics on crime in the public sphere attract more attention than figures on violence in the home. People tend to fear danger in the streets and lament and condemn rising crime rates in society, but often ignore the reality of abuse in the home.

As the truth about domestic violence is revealed, it is becoming indisputable that women and children are not necessarily safe even in the apparent security of their homes. In many contexts all over the world the family, far from being a place where men, women and children live in an atmosphere of shared understanding, respect and love, has supported patriarchal forms of domination and power. The culture of patriarchal domination and violent retribution against any expression of what the dominant person considers rebellion or dissent finds expression in various forms of physical and sexual abuse of women by men in their homes in all societies and among all peoples.

In a bid to preserve the myth that the family is and always will be a safe unit within the community, many people prefer not to pay attention to the startling details of violence in the family now emerging.

In many societies, it is considered "normal" if a man beats his wife, even by most medical health professionals. However, if a woman dares to retaliate with violence she is treated as "mentally abnormal". Only recently have medical professionals recognized the existence of the "battered wife syndrome", a term coined by a US psychologist in 1984 to explain the behaviour of abused victims.

Tolerance of domestic violence manifests itself in warped cultural practices and attitudes. There is an old Hindi saying: "A woman is like spit. Once spat out, she cannot be taken back." In many Asian societies, a woman is conditioned from the moment she is born into accepting that her only purpose in life is to be married and to stay married at all costs. This implies submissiveness to a man no matter how cruel or violent he may be. Most societies have similar written or unwritten expectations of women.

For social workers, lawyers and counsellors trying to deal with domestic violence, one of its most perplexing and difficult features is the inability of many abused women to make a break from their violent home environment because they are bound by strong emotional ties to the abuser. Studies show that battered women tend to return to a violent relationship many times over before leaving for good and making their lives in a safe environment. In many cases, a woman is unable to name the violence in her life. Maybe she is too proud to acknowledge that her marriage is not working. Maybe she is hoping against hope that the repeated promises her husband makes to desist from violence will be kept.

Domestic violence takes many forms, including intimidation and threats, economic deprivation, psychological and sexual abuse, often used repeatedly. Physical violence is one tactic used. It may take the form of a single attack, but is often frequent and in some cases even daily. The assumption that such violence happens only among poor and uneducated people or in "dysfunctional" families is a myth. Studies show that a man who regularly batters his wife or partner and children may be a perfect "gentleman" outside the home. He may be a doctor, minister, lawyer, psychologist, teacher or other professional who would never be violent to other men or women in the public sphere. He can control himself outside, but picks a safe target inside the home.

In no context do women "ask" to be beaten or abused. It should be added that in over 95 percent of domestic assaults, the man is the assailant. There are rare cases in which a woman batters a man, and women have been known to retaliate and sometimes even kill their attacker after prolonged years of battering. But violence in the home is overwhelmingly by men against women.

Statistics are available in plenty:
— In South Africa, one adult woman out of every six is assaulted regularly by her mate. In almost half of these cases, the man involved also abuses the woman's children.
— In France, 95 percent of the victims of violence are women, 51 percent of them at the hands of their husbands.

— In Papua New Guinea, 60 percent of the persons murdered in 1981 were women, the majority by their spouses during or after a domestic argument.

In the USA, violence occurs at least once in 67 percent of all marriages.

— In cases of sexual abuse of children in Canada, most assailants are either family members or persons in a position of trust, according to a 1981 survey.[6]

In most societies, the demands of new economic and social realities are changing the role expectations of both men and women. Nevertheless, some old patterns are not easy to get rid of. Even women who have full-time paid jobs outside of the home are expected in most contexts to depend on men socially and economically, while men continue to be dependent on women for domestic services, including a kind of psycho-emotional support sometimes referred to as "tension management". It continues to be the woman's responsibility to create a home atmosphere that will help men to deal with the pressures of the workplace.

As a Canadian church report notes:

The role of tension manager is the domestic task that leaves a woman most vulnerable to violence from her male partner. In fact, violence against women can be seen as an extreme form of tension management in which a woman absorbs with her body and soul tensions generated in the public sphere — tensions which could otherwise be directed in protest against oppression from the established order.[7]

Sexual harassment

Like rape, sexual harassment has been a hidden problem, treated as a joke or blamed on the victim herself. Because of a long history of silence on the subject, many women feel uncomfortable, embarrassed or ashamed when they talk of personal incidents of harassment. They are afraid that it will reflect badly on their character or that they will be seen as somehow inviting the propositions.[8]

A clear and comprehensive definition of sexual harassment has been provided by the General Assembly of the United Presbyterian Church in the USA. It refers to "any unwanted sexual advance or demands (verbal/physical) which are perceived by the recipient as demeaning, intimidating or coercive". Sexual contact that is *unwanted* in the *perception of the recipient* is therefore to be treated as sexual harassment. The need for a more accurate definition of what constitutes sexual harassment arises from the fact that in many countries, the law courts have been ambivalent about it. Only recently has sexual harassment come to be recognized as a form of violence.

In the past, women did not have the courage to challenge the daily irritation experienced at the hands of people with authority over them, particularly in the workplace. Nor would they have defined this as sexual harassment. But due to the impact of the women's movement, more and more women in many societies now refuse to be treated as objects. Recognizing how much it affects their humanity and dignity, they are no longer able to accept harassment without protest.

But it is also true that most women would still prefer to cultivate an immune system that makes them apparently indifferent to any assault on their sensibilities — verbal, psychological or physical. The motto continues to be: pretend nothing happened rather than go through a process that could cause a great deal of personal agony. Women are not sure that they will be believed if they complain of sexual harassment. They may be ridiculed for being prudish or oversensitive, or even blamed for provoking unwanted behaviour. The consequences on their private lives and family situations can be devastating. In most cases, they would rather not speak out because to do so may cost them their jobs. In most societies, laws to protect women are far from adequate. It is difficult to prove that a woman's modesty and psyche have been wounded by inappropriate words or actions.

The preliminary findings of a 1992 research project instituted by the Swiss government office for equality between women and men confirms just how widespread the problem is. The survey included a detailed interview of 558 women working in 25 different companies and agencies in Geneva. Of the women interrogated, 59 percent affirmed that they had been sexually harrassed at work in the preceding two years. Seventy-one percent of these said the harassment had occurred more than once, and 87 percent of those said the same man had harassed them.

Among the causes for complaint were inappropriate comments about women (35 percent), colleagues' attitudes which caused embarrassment (30 percent), ambiguous or embarrassing comments (19 percent), colleagues showing them pornographic material or leaving it out on display (16 percent), unwanted touching (14 percent), sexual blackmail (2 percent), imposed sexual relations (0.7 percent), physical violence (0.4 percent), and rape or attempted rape (0.2 percent). For 81 percent of the women who experienced sexual harassment, the disagreeable situation lasted for more than a year; of these 16 percent complained of daily harassment for more than a year.

Sexual harassment and fear of it exert social control on women. Research has revealed that women unable to act or behave as they wish adopt "self-censuring" behaviour. Women in all situations impose restrictions of time, space, and movement on themselves because they must always be on guard. At the same time, the non-recognition of sexual harassment as a social reality contributes to the maintenance of silence on the subject. The effect is to lead women to believe that sexual harassment is an integral and inevitable part of their work conditions. [9]

Trade unions have not yet been able to deal with incidents of sexual harassment as "crimes against working women", although many studies have shown that the majority of working women experience some degree of harassment at some stage of their working lives. A few years ago, a group of women brought a case of harassment to the attention of the leading trade union in a nationalized bank in Bangalore, India: a man had slapped a woman colleague at work. The union declined to take up the case, saying it was a personal matter between the woman and man concerned and needed to be dealt with in that way.

An International Labour Office (ILO) report on sexual harassment shows just how widespread and global the problem is. But ILO civil rights lawyer Constance Thomas admits that the attempt to examine the scope of sexual harassment in third-world worksites has only now begun. "We think we are going to find an even more serious problem there," she acknowledged. [10]

Rape

The issue of rape has recently received increased attention in connection with its incidence in wars and conflict situations. The use of women's bodies as weapons in conflict causes revulsion in the minds of all right-thinking people. What it does to the psyche of women who are its victims can never be fully understood or adequately responded to. But despite this awareness of the deep wounds caused, there are still attempts to underestimate or deny the seriousness of this crime. As a brochure from a feminist group in Bangalore, India, points out:

> Rape, which is the most aggressive demonstration of unjust power relationships, as a form of personal violence, is physical assault and symbolic of the degradation of woman-kind, but is a violation of the most sensitive part of the female psyche. Susan Brownmiller defines it as a "conscious process of intimidation by which all men keep all women in a state of fear". It is only of late that rape is being viewed as a criminal attack against an individual and specifically a woman. Otherwise, the shocking sentiment implicit even today in the law, besides the attitude of society, is that a woman "asks for it", or in a spirit of condonation states that a rapist is an individual giving in to his natural virility! [11]

Old assumptions and attitudes die hard. Some years ago, the chief minister of an Indian state complained that the media were blowing attacks on women tourists out of proportion. "What is rape after all?" he asked at a public meeting, adding: "In America a rape occurs every minute. It is as common as drinking tea. One drinks tea and commits a rape."[12]

In July 1991, 271 teenage girls were attacked by male classmates at a boarding school in Kenya because they refused to join a strike against the school authorities. Nineteen girls died of suffocation as they tried to hide, and 71 were raped. The comment by the school's deputy principal was revealing: "The boys never meant any harm against the girls," he asserted. "They just wanted to rape." The editor of Kenya's *Weekly Review*, however, condemned the incident:

> The tragedy has underscored the abominable male chauvinism that dominates Kenyan social life. The lot of our women and girls is lamentable. We treat them as second-class beings, good only for sexual gratification or burdensome chores. We bring up our boys to have little or no respect for girls.[13]

Attitudes such as that of the Indian government minister, the Kenyan educator or the man who shot dead 14 young women at the University of Montreal in 1989 because, he said, they were feminists, may be extreme and isolated reactions, but they unfortunately reflect some old and universal assumptions and attitudes. No real change will be achieved unless these are exposed and radically changed. In many countries, law courts have excused perpetrators of crimes against women on the grounds of the woman's past history. From logic it follows that there are some women who can never be raped!

Rape as a weapon of war

The most brutal part of the build-up of private methods of control to repress people's protest movements in many societies is the increasing incidence of sexual violence against women. Newspaper reports of war and other conflict situations, police action or military intervention often include the phrase "and many women were raped". Mass rape has frequently been used as a political or military weapon either to punish or to intimidate those who rebel. The logic here is to hurt the women in order to teach the men a lesson.

More than forty years after World War II, hundreds of women in Korea, the Philippines and other countries are speaking out about the systematic abuse they experienced at the hands of Japanese soldiers during the war. These women were kidnapped and used as "comfort women" for the soldiers' pleasure. Only now have they finally asserted their right to protest that deep humiliation and to demand financial compensation. But, as a Dutch woman testifying in 1992 to the UN Commission on Human Rights in Geneva said, the deep and lasting psychological damage sustained can never really be compensated for or erased. Courageous enough to speak out as one of the victims of this forced prostitution, the woman concluded her statement by asserting that "I have the right, after almost 50 years, not to forgive all those who caused all the pain."

Rape has often been considered as a "normal by-product" of war. An *International Herald Tribune* editorial (8 December 1992) put it starkly: "All wars are alike in at least three particulars: death, destruction and rape." The comment points to the matter-of-fact attitude with which brutality against women in any conflict situation is viewed.

This hard reality hit the world with fresh force in reports emerging in 1992 from the war in the former Yugoslavia. Rape as an inevitable part of the war was openly acknowledged by all sides in the conflict. The *International Herald Tribune* editorial mentioned above, aptly titled "The rape of Bosnia", was written in that context. It quotes a *New York Times* interview with a Serbian fighter, who explained that his commanders had advised him and his companions that raping Muslim women was "good for raising a fighter's morale", and that he had followed their advice several times at a motel used as a prison for Muslim women. He also claimed that he and his fellow fighters routinely killed the women afterwards.

Ecumenical teams of women who visited the former Yugoslavia in 1992 confirmed the veracity of such accounts, as did delegations from the European Community, Amnesty International and the UN Human Rights Commission. Evidence of systematic mass rape as part of the military strategy there was picked up by the media and caused consternation around the world. Not all the raped women were killed, however. Many survived and went to refugee camps around the divided country, and a few were able to tell the world of their pain. In the framework of the "ethnic cleansing" strategy, some had been detained for at least five months after being made pregnant, by which time abortion was illegal. New expressions like "frontline" and "third-party rape", describing public rape as a means of intimidating and demoralizing enemy forces, have been added to the jargon of warfare. Like other weapons, rape too is becoming more sophisticated!

Article 27, paragraph 2 of the Fourth Geneva Convention on the Protection of Civilian Persons in Times of War (adopted in 1949) classifies wartime rape as a serious human rights violation. It states that "women shall be especially protected against any attack on their honour, in particular against rape, enforced prostitution, or any form of indecent assault." In an agreement reached under the auspices of the International Red Cross, all parties in the Yugoslavia conflict undertook to comply with the Convention. Yet the law has been flouted with impunity. Women are demanding the implementation of the Fourth Geneva Convention in order to ensure that rape is considered a war crime. Women who are dehumanized and violated in this and other wars cannot wait another forty years before justice is done!

Amnesty International reports the rape of political prisoners and women imprisoned in conflict situations in India, the Philippines, Bangladesh, Pakistan, Liberia, Mauritius, Uganda, Senegal, Peru, Guatemala, Mexico, Turkey, Greece, Ireland, and Palestine. The report stipulates that:

> Through their failure to institute adequate investigations, prosecutions and procedural safeguards, governments around the world bear full responsibility for the persistence of widespread rape and sexual abuse in custody. Women are entitled to the protection of their fundamental human rights. But many governments clearly regard rape and sexual assault as less serious offences than other human rights violations. This is a particularly frightening prospect when the perpetrators of these rapes are the same policemen and military personnel charged with the protection of the public.[14]

Prostitution

Prostitution, particularly related to tourism, is now being recognized not only as a grave affront to women's being and psyche but also as a form of violence against women. Poor women tend to be the victims of its most ugly and dehumanizing manifestations. The link between prostitution and global economic injustice and the market economy is increasingly recognized, and it was recently said that a poor nation's most marketable commodity is its women, although statistics show that it is now *children* — the most fragile, unorganized and thus exploitable human beings — who are the main targets of prostitution. Writes Jean Fernand-Laurent, the rapporteur of a 1983 UN Economic and Social Council study on the sex trade:

> The movement involves the traffic of poor women towards rich men in all directions. Economic structural adjustment and loan repayments are causing much anguish to

people in the South. Thirty-seven percent of the Philippines annual budget flows from the country to service debts, while poverty is such that 21,000 women work as prostitutes around the US Subic naval base. In situations of poverty, women and children are the first to suffer, and therefore also to seek desperate survival strategies. The sex industry has rapidly become international, profiting from this vulnerability. [15]

In Belgium, for example, an estimated 2000 women are illegally employed in cabarets, and their numbers are rising each year. Of the 1430 work permits granted to "artistes" in Flanders in 1990, 968 were for "go-go" dancers, of whom 290 were from the Dominican Republic, 228 from the Philippines, 77 from Thailand, 42 from Brazil, 34 from Romania, and 30 from the former USSR. Social workers estimate that 30-50 percent of prostitutes in Belgium are non-Europeans. Sex tourism is the flip side of the coin: each year, 10,000 Belgian men travel as sex tourists to Pattaya in Thailand.

A study commissioned by the German government ministry for women shows that of the 222,000 German tourists who travelled to Thailand in 1989, seven out of ten were men and between 50 and 70 percent of them were travelling to Thailand exclusively for sex purposes.

Although prostitution is treated as a crime for foreign women in Germany, roughly half of the country's 2-400,000 prostitutes, in the big cities at least, are non-Germans. Previously they came mainly from Thailand but, over the last three years, more Latin American women have been working as prostitutes in Frankfurt, while women from Poland, the former Czechoslovakia and Hungary are doing likewise in Hamburg and Berlin.

Many of the estimated 20,000 prostitutes in the Netherlands are also foreign women. The Dutch government is developing new policy guidelines on the sex industry and has set up a support centre called the Stichting Tegen Vrouwenhandel (STV). Of the 168 women aged from 16-39 who contacted the centre between 1989 and 1991, 47 were Dominicans, 38 Filipinas, 37 from Thailand, 9 from Poland, Bulgaria and Yugoslavia.

A "Frauen Informationszentrum", an organization working with prostitutes and abused women in Switzerland, counselled 132 women in 1990. Of these 32 were from Brazil, 29 from the Dominican Republic, 25 from Thailand, 7 from Kenya, 6 from the Philippines. Women also came from as far afield as Eritrea, Mozambique, Tahiti, Uganda, Cuba and Colombia. A 1991 study estimates that each year, 25-30,000 Swiss men travelling abroad will indulge in sexual relations with child prostitutes.

Child prostitution is on the increase all over the world. There are estimated to be up to several hundreds of thousands of prostitutes under the age of 16 in Thailand, for example. [16] In many parts of the world, child prostitutes are drawn mainly from indigenous populations. Nearly one-third of the child prostitutes in Taiwan, for instance, are from indigenous communities despite the fact that only 2 percent of the total population are indigenous. [17]

A letter from a Thai child prostitute expresses the pain of millions of girl children being inducted into the sex trade every day:

Dear Daddy and Mom,
I write to you because I miss you… I am not working as a servant, but as a prostitute. Each day I must serve 7-8 men. I can get diseases like VD, TB, AIDS, etc. They threaten to beat me up if I don't do it. They beat up girls who refused them, until they died. They won't take us to be treated because they are afraid that we will run away. Instead they give us two or three tablets… Being a prostitute is like being a bird in a cage. They can't fly away. [18]

Mail-order brides

These are women from poorer nations who are sold as brides, to men in Europe and Australia in particular. The practice is now being recognized as a new form of violence against women. Women from the South are advertised as "exotic, graceful, beautiful, loyal, reliable," but also "submissive, good with children, not too independent, from a socially stable environment, morally old-fashioned but with a modern outlook, and protected with a health certificate"! Describing its "merchandise", a British marriage bureau promised that "in selecting a Filipina, you could expect her to be passionate yet faithful, loving and caring, hard-working and with none of the hangups in attitudes prevalent in European women."[19]

In 1987, some 200 German agencies were advertising mail-order brides.[20] Marriage bureaus make use of the three-month tourist visa to bring women picked from a catalogue to Germany. Several agencies then offer a "trial period" before a final decision is reached! Prices vary considerably depending on the woman's country of origin. Central and eastern European women are available at the cheapest rate. A Munich agency charges 3500 marks to make contact with a woman from Hungary, Bulgaria or the former Czechoslovakia, and includes her travel costs. If the client does not want to marry her within six months, 50 percent of the fee is returned.

Swiss agencies also offer mail-order bride services and men may also return the women should they prove "unsuitable". It costs between 5-7000 Swiss francs — what one would pay for a good second-hand car — to order a wife from the Philippines. Half of the 28 mail-order brides who sought counsel at the Frauen Informationszentrum in 1989 were being subjected to violence and abuse. Of these 22 had to be treated for injuries resulting from beatings, and had been sexually abused and/or raped.

Other forms of violence that deeply affect the well-being and even survival of women in different contexts are being identified. Among them are some medical techniques, including the invasive power of reproductive technologies, the sex-specific torture of women prisoners, violent attacks on female political and human rights activists, incest and other forms of child abuse including female infanticide, dowry-related violence and even murder, cultural practices like female circumcision and self-immolation by widows, ritual abuse particularly of girl children and the continuing practice of witch-hunting, distorted images of women in the media, advertising and pornography, gang rapes and rape in marriage. Women of colour and other women exposed to rising racial hatred and discrimination are the particular targets of violence. In a recent interview, Dalit women's activist Ruth Manorama said that more than 80 percent of women raped in India are from this oppressed community.

Covert forms of violence

There are more subtle and elusive forms of violence against women that cannot be counted in hard statistics. These include the living deaths millions of women face in their homes, workplaces and other social contexts where they are subjected to discriminatory and dehumanizing attitudes to them *as* women. Such attitudes may be expressed in cruel taunts and harassment that devalue women, denying their right to an opinion, suppressing their desires, locking them into the drudgery of domestic labour, and diminishing their creativity and self-esteem.

Such covert violence is rarely taken seriously. Women are advised not to "over-react" to what are considered "normal" attitudes and to behaviour that is sometimes said to be unconscious and not intended to cause discomfort or pain. But some women are asserting that any form of violence, be it verbal, psychological, emotional or physical, is dehumanizing and therefore unacceptable. They recognize that any attitude or behaviour that reduces women to the level of targets of abuse or harassment is violence. They are demanding that *all* forms of violence from the most blatant to the most subtle be challenged and combatted. Around the world, the women's movement has given them the courage and the space to articulate a vision of life free from violence, where all may contribute, and everyone's gifts may be respected and allowed to flourish.

2. No Longer Silent

My comrade
Just a minute!
Before you strike my cheek with your uplifted hand,
Just think for a minute!

Was your hand lifted
Against the industrialist
Who sucked your life out
Making you work for more than eight hours a day
For a pittance?
No, it wasn't!

Was your hand lifted
Against the politician/leader
Who made a thousand promises
During all the past election campaigns
But quickly forgot you and his promises?
No, it wasn't!

But you lift your hand against me
Just because a cup of coffee has gone cold!

You, who allowed your humanity to be trampled on
So as to ensure your next meal,
You who allowed your humanity
To be debased.
Are you going to debase my humanity
Just for a cup of coffee?

My comrade,
Before you strike my cheek
With your uplifted hand,
Just think for a minute!

Subadhra
(Translated from the original Tamil)

Subadhra's voice expresses women's efforts to reclaim their right to violence-free lives. All over the world, women are recognizing that for too long they have remained silent while their bodies and souls have been the innocent targets of violence and are saying: "Enough is enough!" All over the world such expressions of courage and resistance offer signs of hope.

A few years ago, I met a newly-married woman who was being battered by her husband on just about any pretext. When she told her mother and grandmother about the agony she was going through, they advised her to go back to her husband and learn to tolerate his violence. "All these years, your father and grandfather ill-treated us too," they said. "We took it silently. You too must learn how to accept this. It's our fate for having been born women." Luckily, this young woman was aware that there were other options open to her. She was convinced that she could live alone and take care of herself and therefore did not have to continue submitting to humiliation and violence. After many attempts to heal her marriage, she reluctantly but firmly opted out of the abusive relationship. But millions of women around the world stay imprisoned in painful and sometimes even dangerous home environments.

Over the past two decades, the women's movement has brought into sharp focus the various dimensions and extent of the violence women experience in society, the workplace and the public domain as well as in the supposedly safe setting of their homes. The truth revealed has empowered other women to recognize that they need not bear silently the blows of a dehumanized society that systematically condones and even legitimizes violence. The movement has created a space and climate in which women can tell their stories of physical and mental intimidation and express their pain.

Women have devised various ways to create a secure world for themselves. Subadhra, whose poem I quoted above, and thousands of women like her use poetry, song, drama and street theatre and other creative media to get their message across. In every region of the world, audiovisuals, comic books and simple booklets have been produced as educational tools to help women teach their sisters to protest, resist and protect themselves against increasing violence.

Educational materials like those prepared by the Nicaraguan Association of Rural Workers are an example of such work. Since 1983, the association has made awareness-raising on women's rights among its members, both male and female, one of its principal goals. Using pictures of typical work and family situations, women farmworkers teach small groups of men and women to reflect on their lives. Issues discussed include sexual harassment in the workplace and physical and psychological abuse in the home.

A Namibian group concerned by rising crime rates against women runs workshops and training programmes to improve legal knowledge and organizing skills so that women may be prepared to deal with violence. The project includes neighbourhood women's support groups to ensure that women are trained to understand the social mechanisms creating violence, and learn to develop strategies to deal with it.

The "All Women's Action Movement" (AWAM) in Kuala Lumpur, Malaysia, has helped raise public awareness on the extent of domestic and other forms of violence against women in Malaysian society. Their action pack on legal reforms includes illustrated stories of women who have sought refuge or legal redress, a list of state legal offices to which women may turn, and examples of constructive action by victims and their support groups.

Posters on billboards across the city, in buses and trams, plus a city-wide mailing were part of a massive educational campaign on rape organized in Geneva, Switzerland, by "Viol Secours", a rape crisis centre, in 1992. The campaign message was simple: "Silent acceptance or resistance? How are *you* going to respond to sexual violence?" The telephone number and address of the shelter was supplied. Primarily, the campaign offered a helping hand to women threatened by violence (who are often unable to escape because they do not know whom to trust or depend on). But the campaign message was also addressed to all women as well as to men.

A "Women and Law" committee in Papua New Guinea has done intensive educational work on the issue of domestic violence. PNG statistics are alarming: 43 percent of people killed by violence in 1979 were women; by 1981 the figure had risen to 61 percent. The committee distributed thousands of leaflets and posters explaining that wife-beating is against the law, and produced a television video for people who cannot read that suggested positive ways to build a violence-free community. As efforts in PNG focus on appointing more women as village magistrates, the committee is attempting to educate the magistrates on how to deal with domestic violence. Thanks to its efforts, police personnel now receive compulsory training on how to act with regard to domestic assaults. The committee is realistic enough to know that the police, in spite of their training, will not be at the forefront in tackling domestic violence in rural areas. But it sees such training as an important step towards convincing rural people that wife-beating is indeed wrong.

One of the best educational resources on the subject is a comprehensive and beautifully illustrated manual on "Sexual and domestic violence: Help, recovery and action in Zimbabwe", compiled by Jill Taylor and Sheelagh Stewart in 1991. Research in Zimbabwe had made it obvious that victims must have access to support at the local community level. The manual provides detailed information on the different kinds of support available to the victims of sexual assault and domestic violence, including medical and legal action, and contains a similarly detailed section on counselling victims, including children. Violence against women is defined as a crime, and as a social problem calling for social action including education, training, organizing, and lobbying for change. In a foreword to the manual, Edmund Kahari, the district public relations officer of the Zimbabwe police force, acknowledges that:

> We know that the figure of reported rapes (in 1970, 576 rapes and 17,646 sexual assaults) represents only a fraction of the number of rapes actually committed during the year. The situation regarding wife-beating is equally alarming. We all need to take these problems very seriously. We should try to equip ourselves to help individual victims as well as working to change attitudes towards these crimes.

A similar handbook produced by the Aboriginal and Torres Strait Islander Congress in Australia on "Family violence through black eyes" recognizes that family violence crept into the life of aboriginal communities after colonization. It clearly documents the seriousness of the current situation and analyzes both the causes and possible solutions. The handbook lists possible options for women and abused children, including available legal protection, and proposes a simple workshop to enable communities to deal with the problem of family violence.

Manuals like these are valuable resources in many countries and contexts. Such educational work is rooted in awareness that most societies are uninformed about the different aspects of violence against women and are therefore unable to devise adequate responses. A shocking lack of knowledge of legal provisions is apparent even in "enlightened" societies where women in particular often do not realize that they *can* seek legal redress. In countries with high levels of illiteracy among women, much energy has been devoted to developing simple educational materials to demystify, decode and provide easy access to legal provisions and procedures.

Engagement in educational work has also led women to discover that even where laws for redress do exist, they are ridden with loopholes. It has encouraged them to challenge not only tardiness in implementation but also the flaws that make such laws ineffective to curb violence. The way forms of violence are defined is often ambiguous, as is the definition of consent. More seriously, the will to punish those guilty of violence against women is often lacking. Such crimes, however violent and dangerous, are frequently viewed and condoned as "domestic disputes that should be resolved amicably". Even more serious is the fact that a woman's past history is still, in this day and age, drawn into the debate.

Over the past twenty years, women in many countries have been campaigning for changes in existing laws or for new ones, and rape and family laws and criminal procedure codes have been revamped as a result. But women are aware that this is not enough. Patriarchal attitudes run deep, and the necessary attitudinal changes have not yet occurred.

Devising new ways to deal with violence

Some novel methods of dealing with violence have emerged over the past few decades. In Manitoba, Canada, native American people are using a *circle of healing* to address violence in their communities. Five or six women who began meeting secretly to share their own problems soon realized that they had to extend their work to other women who were also in need of healing. The group connected the psychological, emotional and physical violence directed against them to the economic, social and political underdevelopment of their community. They realized that unless violence against women was dealt with, their communities could not move forward.

In the circle of healing, the entire community is treated to exorcize the pervasive illness of violence. The key to the circle's healing power is a special gathering where the victim, the abuser, community and family members come together to face the situation and the abuser must publicly acknowledge his crime. Members of the community tell the abuser how they feel about what has happened, and offer their support for healing. They also talk to the victim and the families involved. The abuser is given a "healing contract" setting out the punishment — usually community work — and arrangements are made to protect the victim. When the contract expires, a cleansing ceremony takes place to symbolize the return of balance to the abuser, the family and the community. At this point, the healing is complete and the crime can be forgotten. Such healing can take years.

Since the 1970s, women have asserted their right to safety on the streets at any time of day or night. Every year in late September at *Take back the night* marches around the world, but mainly in the West, women name the violence that is the source of their fears, thus refusing the enforced silence long used to cloak the reality. The marches are another attempt to create space for women to speak the truth. Their message is their determination to fight back. This includes demanding safety measures, organizing women's self-defence, lobbying for adequate funding for services to women victims, and public education on the issues involved. Although the marches started from the demand to be able to walk on the streets alone at night, the whole spectrum of violence against women has been highlighted in recent years and the links between racism, homophobia and violence against women exposed.

The Philippines-based Asian Women's Human Rights Commission has *widened the scope of human rights* by insisting that all forms of violence against women — sex tourism, dowry deaths and other forms of domestic violence, pornography, rape, sex-specific forms of torture — are violations of human rights. Among their public awareness-raising strategies are fact-finding missions to trouble areas, international public hearings on Asian women's human rights cases, tribunals on women's issues, and a "declaration on human rights of women of the South". The commission has supported the struggle of Korean "comfort women" (forced to "service" Japanese soldiers during World War II) to obtain adequate compensation.

When Peruvian women in some Lima neighbourhoods demonstrated directly in front of houses where domestic violence was known to have occurred, the incidence of wife-abuse dropped slightly. This technique has been used by women in many contexts in the South, particularly in remote villages where they know that they have only each other to rely on for protection.

In India too, when it was becoming clear that neither the police nor the law courts would protect women who were murdered for dowry (the cases often being registered as suicides), women likewise took matters into their own hands by demonstrating in front of homes where dowry murders had taken place, in order to shame the family into acknowledging its guilt. As well as making clear their determination to deal with individual perpetrators of violence, women have also found ways of protecting their sisters against violence before it happens. In some Indian villages, each woman is given a whistle. The moment she blows it is a signal to other women that she is threatened and needs their support. Then they run to her rescue, threatening the abuser until he stops.

Outdoor theatre dramatizing the different forms that violence against women can take is the methodology used by the "Groundwork Theatre Action Company" and "Teens in Action" in Kingston, Jamaica. In one of the situations they portray, a young girl pleads with her father not to "do that" to her while her mother is away. After the show, the actors engage the audience in a consciousness-raising discussion. "Sistren" is another Caribbean theatre troupe that uses drama as a medium of education and awareness-raising on women's issues.

In the United States, women at one university started a campaign to denounce "date rapists" by *writing their names on bathroom walls*, and students at another university organized a candlelight vigil to demand greater action on "date rapes".

Over the past two decades, since the need to provide temporary shelter to women whose lives are endangered was recognized, *women's crisis and refuge centres* have opened in many countries. Most battered women do not leave home because they do not know where else to go. Often, they do not want family and friends to know what they are going through, and sometimes they know that the home of a family member or friend is not safe either since the abuser can follow them there. Women who have been raped also need safety.

In some crisis and refuge centres, trained lawyers and counsellors offer legal advice and psychological and medical help. The company of other women who have gone through a similar trauma can be highly therapeutic. In such centres, a newcomer may feel she has finally found real understanding and genuine support. By talking with and listening to others, she understands that she is not alone. Slowly, she identifies with others and begins to develop self-esteem, along with the hope that she too can free herself and change her relationships with others.

Women's refuge centres are now being set up in almost every country in the world, sometimes with state support. Often, however, they are managed on shoestring budgets, and are unable to give the full support that all who come to them deserve. Sometimes they must turn women away. The state, the church and the community have not yet realized how important it is for women to sustain each other in this way. Shelters are seen as more institutions whose infrastructure needs to be maintained. The fact that they are usually run on a voluntary basis by women who give their time and energy to provide a haven of support for other women is forgotten. For women whose bodies and souls have been wounded by violence, they may be the only hope.

By daring to identify the various forms of violence they experience and taking steps to end it, women are declaring that they will be passive victims no longer. Over the past two decades, women of all sectors, in urban and rural settings, of all religious persuasions and races, in all nations and regions have been transcending the paralyzing emotions felt by being the victims of forces beyond their control, and are initiating creative action for change. A slogan, "the personal is political", has given them the power to transform their pain into political power in order to usher in a world of greater justice and peace.

Hong Kong feminist theologian Kwok Pui Lan tells the story of two powerful women — Zhang Zhi-xin of China, and Suk Wah of Korea — who suffered greatly at the hands of the state. Describing how they were transformed by their experiences, she commented: "In the struggle of Asian people... many Zhi-xins and Suk Wahs must have heard the cry of the people and felt their pain... They are one with the people and their hearts are touched by their pain. It is this passion that makes them identify with the exploited, that motivates and empowers them to rectify wrong, to fight for justice."[21]

Sharadamma comes from a lower middle-class background and lost her daughter on the altar of greed for more dowry. For a long time, she could not believe what had happened, or that she would never see justice done because the police had been bribed and the case registered as a suicide. Sharadamma, a simple Indian woman struggling to keep her family going, was suddenly confronted with grave injustice. She describes this as a conversion experience: since then she has devoted her life to work with women and the families of women murdered in family violence. Here are three verses from an epitaph from a mother to her murdered daughter that Sharadamma inspired me to compose:

O daughter of mine,
I loved you.

When you said you would not go back,
Pleaded with me, cried endless tears,
Showed me the scars of the wounds he had inflicted on you,
I knew you would die.
But I closed my eyes, my ears, my heart to your entreaties.
Believe me,
I loved you.

O daughter of mine,
I love you.
You lie there a heap of lifeless ashes.
I feel the pain you bore as the flames devoured you.
I hear with terror your shrill cries of pain.
Forgive me my now-useless tears,
My lack of courage, my silence when I should have spoken.
Believe me,
I love you.

O daughter of mine,
I love you,
For a woman you have made of me.
No longer will I remain entombed in silence.
No longer will my daughter or any other daughter burn.
I thank you for teaching me the power of womanhood.
Believe me,
I love you, I love you, I love you... [22]

It is in this sense that the women's movement of the past 20 years represents "not merely an oppositional force fuelled by anger, a rather negative reaction to oppression, but the development of a distinctive female culture, a positive creative force inspiring men and women alike". [23]

This shift has encouraged concerned and sensitive men in all parts of the world to confront their own sexuality and abuse of power, and to support women in their struggles. Michael Kaufman, an educator on male violence, describes men's dilemma in this way:

At the individual level, the best way to show yourself and the world that you have power and control is by exercising it around you, over those human beings who are defined as not having any, that is, women and children. Violence becomes a terrific means for a man to say to himself that he is a man because he can dominate someone who clearly is not.

The violence and power of individual men is based on their social power, but also on their very real terror, real isolation, real alienation and real fear, which recreate the need for them to control others. The social power of men creates the possibility to act on that need. [24]

Just as women have for centuries denied themselves freedom by seeking refuge in internalized self-abnegation, so men have sought refuge in institutions and structures of domination, not least of all military power, in order to avoid having to face up to their fears.

Michael Kaufman is hopeful that real change is possible. Men can use their influence to ensure that stricter penalties against violence are applied. They can promote peaceful solutions to conflict in every sphere of life, including international relations. Men can develop skills of relating, caring and bonding based on love and commitment to the other.

Small groups of men in solidarity with women, seeking their own liberation as they give moral support to women who are discovering theirs, have sprung up in many parts of the world. These groups are signs of hope whose importance should not be underestimated. Women cannot be held responsible for "educating" men into new patterns of respect and relationship. It is up to the men.

Other signs of hope

It is important to recognize that some governments are taking positive action, reviewing existing laws to ensure that victims have access to legal redress. Of course, the struggle for full and comprehensive legal protection must continue as long as the pain women experience continues to be trivialized in police stations and law courts. But there has been considerable progress in many countries thanks to women's valiant efforts to ensure justice.

The UN Commission on the Status of Women at its March 1991 meeting in Vienna continued to press for further action on this issue. A Canadian resolution recommended the creation of an international instrument to address the issue of violence against women in all its forms, and called upon the UN Division for the Advancement of Women (DAW) to convene a meeting of experts to that end.

The call was repeated at a meeting convened by the Organization of American States in Caracas, Venezuela, in August 1991. Considering the viability of an inter-American convention on women and violence, the meeting agreed that:

> It would be highly advisable to undertake the development of an international instrument to deal with the general typification of gender-specific manifestations of violence, the obligation of states in this area, a definition of minimal rights and remedies to be afforded and the mechanisms to ensure the foregoing. The participants agreed that the suggested convention should address the issues of prevention, punishment and eradication of violence against women in its different manifestations. [25]

On the recommendation of its Commission on the Status of Women, the UN Economic and Social Council (ECOSOC) on 30 May 1991 (in resolution 1991/18) urged member states to adopt, strengthen and enforce legislation prohibiting violence against women, and to take appropriate administrative, social and educational measures to protect women from all forms of physical and mental violence.

High-level representatives of governments, non-governmental organizations and the UN system in five Andean countries (Bolivia, Colombia, Ecuador, Peru and Venezuela) participating in a strategic planning conference organized in Quito in October 1991 by the UN Development Fund for Women, declared that preventing violence against women is a development priority. The declaration recognizes that "violence against women is a universally acknowledged problem" as well as being "one of the most serious obstacles to the enhancement of the living conditions and participation of women" in Latin America and the Caribbean. "Acts of violence against women are a clear violation of basic human rights," the declaration noted.

Ministers from 16 western European nations meeting in Brussels in March 1991 issued a set of 30 specific recommendations to their governments in which they committed themselves "to stimulate all members of concerned governments to pay particular attention to problems related to physical and sexual violence against women". Future meetings are to deal with issues such as violence against children and young girls, prostitution, pornography, the sex trade, physical and sexual violence among minority groups, and sexual harassment in the workplace.

In 1991, the European Community Commission proposed the adoption of a code of conduct prohibiting sexual harassment in the workplace throughout the Community. The proposal is a non-binding recommendation to governments rather than a directive requiring legislation in all 12 countries. The code broadly defines sexual harassment as "unwanted conduct of a sexual nature or other conduct affecting the dignity of women and men at work". It advises employers, unions and employees on practical prevention measures, including publication of workplace standards that expressly forbid sexual harassment, diligent internal investigation of complaints, and formal disciplinary procedures. Research in several EC member-states showed that certain groups, including divorced women, homosexuals, new employees, minorities, and women assigned to non-traditional tasks, are particularly vulnerable to harassment. [26]

Both governmental and nongovernmental organizations in the Caribbean have begun to address the question of violence against women by opening crisis centres, shelters, support networks, and legal aid clinics. State desks whose primary purpose is to assist the victims of sexual abuse are another sign that governments in the region are beginning to take this problem seriously; several states have amended their laws while model legislation on sexual offences is being considered by CARICOM governments.

Of course, there is a wide gap between governments' and international organizations' stated goals and plans and what happens in women's daily lives. Statistics in fact show that in spite of all government claims, violence against women is on the increase, and the state in many instances has been party to the violation of women's basic survival rights.

Violence against women: a human rights issue

For the past two years, women around the world have been organizing "Sixteen days of activism against gender violence". Beginning on November 25 (the International Day Against Violence Against Women declared by Latin American and Caribbean feminists to commemorate the brutal murder of two sisters in the Dominican Republic in 1960), and ending on December 10 (the anniversary of the 1948 Universal Declaration of Human Rights), the "Sixteen days" includes World AIDS Day (December 1) and the anniversary of the Montreal massacre of fourteen women college students (December 6). The campaign seeks to highlight the universal existence of gender violence, create awareness that it violates human rights, and empower women to take leadership on this issue.

During the 1991 "Sixteen days", hundreds of women's groups around the world sponsored public demonstrations, panels, meetings with authorities and policy-makers, radio and television programmes, petition drives, special editions of newsletters, and poster campaigns to protest gender violence. A worldwide petition drive calling on the UN World Conference on Human Rights (Vienna, June 1993) to focus on women's human rights collected more than 200,000 signatures. Addressed to the UN secretary-general, the petition urged the Conference (the first of its kind in 25 years) to expand the definition of human rights violations to include gender violence.

In an opening statement to a February 1992 UN workshop on "Global strategies for achieving gender fairness in the courts: Eliminating violence against women", the UN under-secretary-general for human rights, Jan Martensen, affirmed:

> The issue of violence against women is a growing concern of the UN. The Nairobi "Forward-Looking Strategies for the Advancement of Women to the Year 2000" [formulated by the End-UN Women's Decade meeting there in 1985] reflects the international community's recognition that violence against women exists in various forms in everyday life in all societies. Such violence is a major obstacle to the achievement of peace and other objectives of the UN.
>
> ...I [have] underlined the importance of a holistic approach to human rights... [since] decisions in many areas of activity have an impact on respect for the human rights of women and, in turn, respect for women's rights will positively affect the rights of others. It has become evident that the promotion of enjoyment of human rights of women must be an integral part of our whole approach of promoting human rights. [27]

Whether the commitment with which Mr Martensen credits the UN will be reflected in its work remains to be seen. Amnesty International has been more specific about what needs to be urgently done. Its "Twelve steps to protect women's human rights" include the prevention and punishment of rape, sexual abuse and other ill-treatment by government agents; persecution because of family connections; ill treatment of women refugees, asylum-seekers and women from ethnic minorities; judicial and extrajudicial executions, "disappearances", and the death

penalty. Other necessary steps are provision of adequate
health care for all detainees and prisoners; immediate and
unconditional release of all prisoners of conscience;
prompt and fair trials for all political prisoners; protection
of women's human rights in situations of armed conflict;
ratification of international human rights instruments, and
support for the work of relevant intergovernmental organizations.

Amnesty asserts that:

> Governments are responsible yet often fail to take action
> to prevent human rights abuses. The international commu-
> nity can play a decisive role in protecting human rights
> through vigilant and concerted action. Important steps
> towards protecting women's human rights worldwide
> include documenting human rights violations, publicizing
> these as widely as possible, and campaigning to press
> government authorities for an end to the abuses. Govern-
> ments which fail to protect fundamental human rights should
> be confronted with the force of international public
> opinion.[28]

But even Amnesty has failed to view *all* forms of
violence against women as human rights violations. In the
meantime, violence is a routine experience for women in
every nation, causing untold suffering and despair.
Behind the statistics are individuals — women whose
bodies and souls are deeply wounded by rape, sexual
assault, abuse and battery, each a victim of forces beyond
her control.

3. Whither the Church?

The World Council of Churches strives to bring together a community of solidarity and mutual concern where faith and principles are expressed in appropriate action. Such a community will not accept violence against women, which is an intolerable manifestation of unequal power relations between women and men. When human sin breaks the trust in this community, Christians are called to assist, to be Christ present for those who struggle for their dignity and rights, to manifest concern for the welfare of others and loving kindness to people in need. A fundamental respect for each human being includes a commitment to the rights and dignity of women. [29]

There are many stories of broken trust within the Christian community. A few years ago, we heard of a woman whose pastor husband made a habit of beating her and then going out with other women. On a friend's advice, she complained to the bishop of her church. He suggested that she call on him if it happened again. Yet when she did phone him, late at night, the bishop asked: "How do I know you are telling the truth?"

At one theological college in India, young men being trained for ministry claimed their "cultural right" to beat their wives! There was also the case of the Indian lay preacher who left his young wife and child to go to Africa to do "the Lord's work". A few months later, he wrote expressing deep concern because he would have to desert her. God had spoken to him and asked him to marry a woman who worked with him...

Church statements condemning violence against women are still few and far between, or are incorporated into other statements so that the specificity of women's experiences of abuse does not get the attention it deserves. Furthermore, although some voices have been raised against clergy misconduct and domestic violence over the past ten years and some churches have acted on the issue, much remains unsaid and the churches have been slow to express their concern.

Sexual harassment and abuse in church contexts or at ecumenical gatherings is a fact to be recognized and roundly condemned. It is imperative that every Christian denomination discuss it and prepare adequate theological and pastoral responses.

Strong pressure from women in its member churches to do something concrete on the issue led the World Council of Churches (WCC) in 1991 to appoint a task-force on violence against women. Composed of five men and five women, it meets regularly and has produced a pastoral/educational brochure (quoted at the beginning of this chapter) which is now available in the Council's four official languages, and is distributed to all participants at WCC-organized meetings and conferences. In the pipeline is a series of seminars to prepare WCC staff to deal with possible cases of sexual harassment at such meetings. A clause stating that "sexual harassment and all forms of related violence will not be tolerated or condoned and offenders will be held responsible for their behaviour, and will be subject to appropriate disciplinary action" was incorporated in the WCC staff rules and regulations in 1993.[30]

In spite of some attempts to challenge the churches to action, domestic violence or clergy sexual misconduct with trusting parishioners are still taboo subjects in many nations in the South. The churches in these countries too have, by and large, maintained silence on the issue. Musimbi Kanyoro, executive secretary for women in church and society with the Lutheran World Federation, reports that:

> Even though women in North America and to a lesser extent in Europe are beginning to speak out about sexual harassment, there is still much reluctance in many societies in the world to discuss issues of sexual violence openly. Many women who have been victims of violence feel guilty because they have been socialized to believe that they provoke men's violence towards them.[31]

In many nations of the South, women see a clergyman as akin to God. When their basic trust in a pastor and, through him, in the church, is broken, most women are too afraid and shocked to accuse the perpetrator of the violence. That sexual harassment and abuse by clergy and pastoral counsellors exists in all regions of the world, and that the churches will have to deal with it, must be acknowledged. Kanyoro emphasizes that:

> It is only in the recent past that churches have begun discussions on this topic. The rude discovery that even church ministers are violent to women challenges the church to overcome the temptation to be trapped in its own culture. The righteousness of the church must include social responsibility as well as individual morality... If the church does not speak out against violence inflicted on women, then by its silence and non-action it is compromising its prophetic call. [32]

Some churches *have* responded. The following sampling of policy positions, training and workshop manuals and guidelines for redress all indicate that there is hope that the church will and can tackle this problem.

The *Canadian Conference of Catholic Bishops* in a 1991 statement entitled "To live without fear", declared that "violence against women breaks the fifth commandment. It is a sin, a crime and a serious social problem... Helpful, compassionate and just responses to women who are victims of violence are important and needed. Long-term strategies for prevention are critical."

The *Anglican Church of Canada* has an excellent report, prepared by its taskforce on violence against women and presented to its general synod in 1986, that focuses on wife abuse. The report holds that "many Christians remain unaware of the extent to which the church has been implicated in condoning and even supporting the behaviour of husbands when they physically punished their wives. Indeed, the church defined such 'discipline' as the bounden duty of a husband in order to correct his wife's soul. A second reason Christians should take pains to confront this particular form of abuse is that theological legitimization has served to reinforce other cultural rationalizations, such as 'a man's home is his castle', so that wife-battering has been trivialized and rendered invisible."

A *United Church of Canada (UCC)* statement against sexual harassment in the church provides clear guidelines for action by employers and institutions to deal with victims and victimizers. A UCC educational brochure entitled "Women in abusive relationships: The church has been silent for too long" lists some of the causes, and suggests that "religion alone is not responsible for such a catalogue of evils, but it contributes to them and even blesses them at times. Change comes slowly and the churches have not been leaders in bringing it about. Our concerns have been the sanctity of the family, reconciliation, restoring marriages, when often the first need is for an end to violence, for safety for women and children and for justice for the oppressed." The brochure indicates what abused women need and what each person or congregation can do in response.

The general assembly of the *Presbyterian Church (USA)* has adopted its own policy and procedures on sexual misconduct. A policy statement makes clear that "sexual misconduct is a violation of ministerial, employment and professional relationships and is never permissible." A theological statement on the issue has also been approved. These instruments are intended to "prevent any person from obtaining and maintaining an unwarranted position of power".

The findings of a 1988 study on sexual harassment in the church by the *United Methodist Church* in the USA in which 1578 clergy and lay people, including church workers, college and seminary students participated, revealed the extent of the problem and led to the conclusion that the issue needs urgent attention. A UMC Board of Global Ministries service centre educational packet on ministries with women in crisis suggests possible responses to such violence against women as physical violence, rape, domestic abuse; sexual exploitation (including sexual harassment), prostitution, pornography; economic exploitation; widowhood, divorce, drug and alcohol abuse, depression and imprisonment.

In the Netherlands, the *Reformed Churches in the Netherlands* and the *Netherlands Reformed Church* have agreed that women who experience sexual abuse or harassment within church structures need more help. Pastors across the country are to be specially trained to receive such complaints and carry out confidential investigations, and a preparatory course on "the pastor's role and intimate questions" was held in the fall of 1991. [33]

The *Uniting Church in Australia* with representatives from the *Uniting Aboriginal and Islander Christian Congress* commission on women and men have produced a brochure on sexual violence in the church community entitled "Break the silence... and the truth shall set you free".

The Latin American Council of Churches department of women's and children's ministries has produced illustrated booklets on violence against women and children as part of an effort to educate congregations on the extent of the problem, and provide guidelines on what Christian communities can do to support victims.

At the VIth assembly of the *All Africa Conference of Churches* in Harare, Zimbabwe, in October 1992, a young woman theologian from Kenya delivered a powerful and very moving sermon on what the kingdom of God means in the context of violence, thereby creating one of the rare occasions when the attention of a major church gathering has focused on this topic!

"Violence is promoted by greed for power and money, desire to dominate and control others," Nyambura

Njoroge said. "It is easy to identify with the violence committed during civil wars and against nature... But I want us to challenge ourselves on the violence and wars that begin right in our bedrooms... the domestic violence that is experienced by women and children in our homes." Njoroge also described unscientific abortion practices, particularly in the context of teenage pregnancies, as "violence against God's creation", and rape as "another violence which is not taken seriously".

The family: a safe place for women and children?

The question of whether the family is a safe place for women and children has to be asked and answered, particularly by the church which has placed so much emphasis on the sacrament of marriage and on family life.

Women have always been the backbone of family life and have held families together in the midst of tensions and changes. And yet, when a woman wishes to opt out of an abusive relationship, she is blamed for breaking the family unit! Confronted with cases of women and children exposed to danger in their homes, fear of violating the sacrament of marriage and the ideal of Christian family life has often paralyzed the churches into inactivity. Both church and community have turned a blind eye to the reality of such situations on the pretext that no one has the right to interfere in a couple's private life.

The subtle message conveyed is that family life is a woman's responsibility and that nothing justifies family breakup. A Canadian woman testifies:

> I was active in the church throughout the 20 years of my marriage, during which I lived in constant fear. I was told by the church that, as a Christian, I was responsible for my children, my husband, my marriage. In fact, whatever happened in the home was my responsibility... The church was my lifeline... It was the only place my husband allowed me to go... But these messages helped me stay in that relationship of fear for a long time. [34]

This testimony reminded me of an Indian woman who suffered daily battering by her husband for nine years. Describing her marriage, this woman explained:

> He was a leader in the church community, serving on the pastorate committee and diocesan council. No one would believe me when I said that this "gentleman" was nearly killing me. We went to church regularly and he would watch me all the time — whom I spoke to and what I did. He remained in the pastorate committee even after I escaped from him, and the bishop has been urging me to reconcile with this man of whom I am so afraid.

Christian women's initiatives

Knowing that it is often difficult to come out of an abusive relationship, women have responded with commitment and compassion to their sisters' suffering.

The Women's Inter-Church Council of Canada has designed a very useful workshop as a resource for theological education. Called "Hands to end violence against women", it uses case studies of women who have experienced violence, examines myths and realities around the issue, analyzes the factors that encourage violence, and suggests action strategies for a community approach to this pervasive evil.

One of the best known and most effective campaigners in this field, who has done extensive work on sexual abuse in the church, Marie M. Fortune directs a centre in Seattle for the prevention of sexual and domestic violence, and many women and denominations in the US and Canada have sought her guidance on how to deal with the issue of sexual misconduct by clergy. The centre received its first call from a victim of sexual abuse by a clergyman in 1983; since then, it has dealt with over 500 cases (averaging three calls a week) from every denomination, and has trained over 2000 religious professionals and leaders from the US and Canada to deal with this concern.

Established in 1987 in Australia, CASA House provides a 24-hour crisis care programme with supportive counselling and public advocacy for women victims. In 1989, several churches funded CASA to do a study on women, the church and sexual violence. The study challenged the church to break its silence on this crime, support the victims and educate the clergy. The next phase of "Project Anna" (so named in honour of the woman who recognized Jesus as the long-awaited liberator) was launched in 1990 to provide an educational and consultative service to the churches on the issue.

In response to a request from women on all sides of the war in the former Yugoslavia, the World Council of Churches in 1992 called on people around the world to wear black on one day of the week as a sign of solidarity and commitment to the raped and violated women there, and in all other wars and conflicts around the world. It is a day not only of mourning but of protest, symbolic of people's determination to struggle for a violence-free world.

4. Women's Theological Visions

> Weep no more my sisters.
> God knows that you weep, and
> She weeps with you.

These words of compassion and comfort were spoken by feminist theologian Elizabeth Bettenhausen in response to what speakers at "the Well", the women's space at the sixth assembly of the World Council of Churches in Canada in 1983, had to say about violence against women. After listening to voices from Palestine, South Africa, Nicaragua, India and Canada, Bettenhausen said that although she could not immediately find words of comfort from the Bible, she could at least share the assurance of God's sorrow over women's tears.

Such faith has empowered women theologians all over the world to seek theological meaning for women's suffering, to go beyond expressing pain to attempting to reconstruct some of the basic theological assumptions that have tended to legitimize it.

In a moving Bible study on rape and patriarchy, for example, WCC deputy general secretary Mercy Oduyoye (a Ghanaian theologian) tells the story of Dinah (Gen. 34) in the latter's own words:

> Being an only daughter and always seeking the company of other daughters, it was in search of companions that I stepped out of my mother's tent. My father had bought land to lay claim to space. I stepped out to claim the space God had given us and to seek the friendship and solidarity of the women of our new neighbourhood.
>
> The brute force that pounced on me and carried me away, kicking and screaming, later took flesh and blood in the person of Shechem, said to be a prince. This royal rapist could not have known who I was, let alone my name. I was but clay in his hands as he pounded and squeezed vigorously until I would yield what would please him. I was just a part of silent nature to be worked until I produced or became what would please men. That I screamed and scratched meant nothing. I was female and should expect to be raped…

Not a word from me is recorded anywhere. That for me is the saddest part. Do I have a say in how my life is managed? Am I and the women I went out to seek just chips on a patriarchal bargaining table?[35]

Oduyoye referred at the start of her Bible study to Phyllis Trible's important contributions to feminist theology. In *Texts of Terror*,[36] Trible traces the lives of four biblical women: Hagar (Gen. 21:9-21), Tamar (2 Sam. 13:1-22), an unnamed concubine (Judg. 11:29-40), and the daughter of Jephthah (Judg. 11:29-40). The stories of these four women who are used, abused, discarded or killed by patriarchal power and lust are virtually unknown, and very few sermons have been preached about their lives. The God of justice and compassion does not intervene to save their lives. Worse, their sacrifice seems to be part of the divine plan.

To Trible and women to whom her hermeneutical model makes sense, these texts of terror are not "relics of a primitive and inferior past" but ring with contemporary overtones. For violated women, God may seem to be absent or strangely silent while the andro-centric Bible, the predominantly male images of God, and the mostly male church hierarchy can symbolize an uncaring church that is blind to the deep pain they experience.

Women hear the silence of the church in distorted teachings and practices, in inadequate preparation of partners for marriage, in one-sided interpretations of biblical passages in the marriage service (like citing Eph. 4:21 as permission for a man to "discipline" his wife to obedience and submission). They hear it in the imposition of a self-effacing docile image of Mary, in liturgy that does not include their experience, in a refusal to believe women's accounts of their own or their sisters' suffering at men's hands.

"Christ suffered and died for you on the Cross. Can't you bear some suffering too?" is a question often addressed, in one form or another, to women when they appeal to the church for succour. Perhaps one of the most pernicious aspects of Christian teaching has been this imposed *theology of sacrifice and suffering*.

A sacrificial lifestyle and a commitment to die for the other are indeed Christ-like qualities that women are willing to continue to emulate in order to protect people's lives and livelihood. Women understand Christ's sacrifice and resurrection as signs of full liberation. As Roman Catholic theologian from the Philippines Mary John Mananzan suggests:

> The experience of the resurrection is the experience of the fully liberated Christ, which is in itself liberating... My experience of liberation in Christ's resurrection also inspires me to continue with courage to struggle with the poor and the oppressed, even in the midst of danger and insecurity, because I have come to understand that it is when I try to save my life that I lose it, and it is by being ready to lose it that I gain it. [37]

But women also ask whether the sacrifice demanded of them has a purpose. As one Indian women's group put it:

> Christ died on the Cross because humankind could not bear his disturbing and uncomfortable message of salvation for the world. By his death, he saved the world from its hypocrisy, apathy and selfishness. He was the scapegoat for a wicked and cruel world. Christ gave of himself for a purpose.
>
> The theology of sacrifice that is thrust on women is of no purpose... Women are the scapegoats of this theology. What they have to discover for themselves is the resurrection element in their sacrifice, as a step towards the discovery of their power. [38]

Arms outstretched as if crucified, the sculpture of the woman by artist Almuth Lutkenhaus-Lackey presently stands on the grounds of Emmanuel College at the University of Toronto. For the women of all faiths and no faith at all who gathered around it in December 1989 to mourn the deaths of 14 brutally murdered Canadian women students, the sculpture expressed the mingling of compassion and suffering of Christ's death.

The 1986 Anglican Church of Canada's taskforce on violence against women report mentioned earlier (see page 42) delves deeper into the concepts of suffering and sacrifice. "Jesus' voluntary suffering and death on the cross cannot and must not be paralleled with the involuntary suffering of women, children or other victims of violence, nor be used to justify their situation in any way."

For Mercy Oduyoye, sacrifice is that which is "freely and consciously made" and is "noble and lovely, loving and motivated by love and gratitude". Violence against women is none of these. "The Christ for me," she says, "is the Jesus of Nazareth who agreed to be God's 'sacrificial lamb', thus teaching that true and living sacrifice is *that which is freely and consciously made*... who approved of the costly sacrifice of the woman with the expensive oil who anointed him in preparation of his burial, thereby also approving all that is noble and lovely, loving and motivated by love and gratitude."[39]

US Methodist ministers Joanne Carlson-Brown and Rebecca Parker take a more radical approach in their ground-breaking article "For God so loved the world":

> Christianity is an abusive theology that glorifies suffering. Is it any wonder that there is so much abuse in modern culture when the predominant image or theology of the culture is of "divine child abuse" — God the Father demanding and carrying out the suffering and death of his own son? If Christianity is to be liberating for the oppressed, it must itself be liberated from this theology.[40]

Black womanist theologian Delores S. Williams takes a similar position:

> My exploration of black women's sources has revealed a heretofore undetected structure of domination... operative in African-American women's lives since slavery. The structure... is surrogacy, and it gives black women's oppression

its unique character, and raises challenging questions about the way redemption is imaged in a Christian context.

God's gift to humans, through Jesus, was to invite them to participate in this ministerial vision ("whosoever will, let them come") of righting relations. The response to this invitation by human principalities and powers was the horrible deed that this cross represents — the evil of humankind trying to kill the ministerial vision of life... Thus, to respond meaningfully to black women's historic experience of surrogacy-oppression, the theologian must show that redemption of humans can have nothing to do with any kind of surrogate role Jesus was reputed to have played in the bloody act that supposedly gained victory over sin/or evil. [41]

For women in violent contexts who have clung to the image of a loving compassionate God and of God's son who so loved the world that he was willing to die for it, such a theological position is difficult to accept. But living in what feminist theologian Mary Hunt calls "a world of contextual violence and episodic justice", we may need to try to understand what it is that these theologians are inviting us to discover. And this may involve looking at violence and the Christian tradition in a more radical way.

Hunt in fact suggests that "those texts, doctrines and practices that perpetuate what today is considered violence, regardless of their historical centrality in the tradition, be dropped". She is aware that she is calling for fundamental change in Christianity when she suggests that "we begin with the basics like the violent death of Jesus, and look fearlessly for alternative ways of articulating meaning and value. Only by doing so," Hunt concludes, "will we be able to say that there is no cause and effect between Christianity and a violent culture, and perhaps in the process we will undo some of the violence. [42]

Clearly, this is a call for a shift from the traditional third-world liberation theology view of the cross. Yet the feeling of oneness with the suffering of Christ has sustained victims of discrimination and oppression for centuries. It assures women that Christ understands if no one else will. Hong Kong feminist theologian Kwok Pui Lan describes the vital significance to Asian women of Christ's suffering:

> It is the person on the cross who suffers like us, was rendered a nobody, who illuminates our tragic existence and speaks to countless women in Asia. We are not looking to Jesus as a mere example to follow, neither shall we try to idolize him. We see Jesus as the God who takes human form and suffers and weeps with us.[43]

Argentinian theologian Nelida Ritchie makes the same point in describing the courage of the "Mothers of the Plaza de Mayo", and a mother's grief when she knows her son has been killed:

> God stands still before such human agony and is moved. Each time the Gospel speaks of human suffering, it shows his (Jesus') complete identification with the other's situation; it shows his creative and active solidarity. Jesus' feelings precipitate changes, a search for the causes, that transform the pain-causing situation.
>
> This ability to "feel with others" leads Jesus to stop hunger, eradicate illness, and remove the burdens that hamper life. His compassion does not stop with saying "Don't cry", but goes on to restore what the person has lost so that tears are replaced by true joy... Resurrection, the giving back of life, like a miracle, is a sign that anticipates the complete transformation for which Christ is responsible. All of us who proclaim the Lordship of Jesus Christ... are called to be in solidarity with those who cry and search, to help restore what is lost to those who mourn.[44]

The final document of the Ecumenical Association of Third-World Theologians intercontinental women's conference (held in Oaxtapec, Mexico, in December 1986) differentiates the suffering that goes with ushering in new life from that which is inflicted by the oppressor and is passively accepted:

Many Christians in our continents are seeking to see in Jesus' suffering, passion, death and resurrection a meaning for their own suffering… Nevertheless, we have a mission to announce that Christ brought new life to humanity and that this was the whole point of his suffering. Suffering that is inflicted by the oppressor and is passively accepted does not lead to life; it is destructive and demonic. But suffering that is part of the struggle for the sake of God's reign or that results from the uncontrollable and mysterious conditions of humankind is rooted in the paschal mystery, evocative of the rhythm of pregnancy, delivery and birth. This kind of suffering is familiar to women at all times, who participate in the pains of birth and the joys of the new creation.[45]

While this is a debate that needs to be pursued, it is clear that senseless suffering can never be legitimized by the cruel death that Christ suffered on the cross. Marie Fortune reminds us that "rather than the sanctification of suffering, Jesus' crucifixion remains a witness to the horror of violence. It is not a model of how suffering should be borne, but a witness of God's desire that no one should have to suffer such violence again."[46]

Another area of Christian teaching that needs to be explored further is that of *forgiving and forgetting*. Women are told that Christ forgave his enemies even as he hung on the cross, beaten and abused by insolent might. But again, the parallel is far from convincing if we think of who violated women are asked to forgive and why.

Some images come to mind. There is the image of the Dutch "comfort woman" forced to "service" Japanese soldiers during World War II who told us that she "had the right not to forgive after 50 years". Or the image of a bruised five-year-old in a slum in Madras who had been raped. Or that of a three-year-old who was sexually abused in a day-care centre by people she and her parents trusted. And there is the image of the woman, mentioned earlier, who had been battered every single day for nine years by her husband, who had lost hearing in one ear, whose arms, legs and breasts bore the tell-tale marks of ruthless violence.

I could not agree more with Mary Hunt when she writes[47] that "such forgiving and forgetting is pathological advice in a culture of violence". The world must understand women's inability to forgive or forget wounds inflicted without meaning on their bodies and souls when no adequate retribution has been made. The glib demand for forgiveness is an injustice, and the traditional emphasis on forgiving and forgetting contributes to an abused woman's oppression. She gives the abuser many chances, covering up for him and pretending that the nightmare is over, hoping that forgiveness will heal the relationship. She is often proved wrong, and sometimes it is too late.

Marie Fortune outlines an ethical framework for dealing with violence against women. Assuming that the basic premise is Micah's admonition to "do justice, love mercy and walk humbly before God" (6:8), she concludes that justice is central to the scriptures and to the church in an attempt to right relationships that are distorted by violence. On that basis:

> Truth-telling, acknowledgment of the violation, compassion, protection of the vulnerable, accountability, restitution and vindication are the requirements for doing justice and mercy in the face of violation and injustice.[48]

Compassion, accountability, restitution and vindication are the norms. Forgiveness comes later:

> Forgiveness is possible in the aftermath of physical abuse only if the person who has been subjected to it has been assured of personal safety, and is no longer subjected to verbal or psychological abuse. Even after all abuse has ceased, forgiveness is a long process. A person recovering from abuse should not be burdened with the unrealistic expectations of a pastoral worker who wants the person to "forgive and forget". Not only the abused person's rights but

their very being has been violated, and they need an opportunity to vent their anger and rage.

Forgiving oneself can be the hardest task for a victim
whose self-image has been shattered... Real forgiveness
comes at the final stage of a long process through which
victims regain control of their lives. [49]

Marie Fortune holds that forgiveness becomes an
option *if* some form of justice is done. The word "vindication" best describes what needs to happen before a victim
is able to forgive. As Fortune points out:

Ultimately, vindication for the victims is the substance of
justice and mercy. Vindication refers not to vengeance and
retaliation but to the exoneration and justification of those
who have experienced harm, made legitimate complaints,
and consequently been imputed. Surely the physical, emotional and spiritual key to healing from violation is to be set
free from the multiple layers of suffering it created. [50]

Many women would assert that the *hierarchical dualism* of Christian theology and ecclesiology has been at the
root of much violence against women. A tradition which
is built on a hierarchy of power relations — God above
humanity, the priest above the congregation, and men
above women — seems to be sanctioning the abuse of
power and makes women in congregations among the
most vulnerable and susceptible to that abuse. To deal
adequately with this issue calls for a new look at ecclesiology as it has been understood and practised. But is the
church ready for this?

The statement by the Presbyterian Church in the USA
cited earlier (see page 43) acknowledges this problem and
suggests the need for an alternative way of dealing with it:

A problem that occurs in traditional procedures for
redressing grievances when it comes to sexual harassment is
that the abuser is most often higher in the hierarchical
structure of the organization than is the abused. This problem also occurs within the structure of the church. As a

result, there needs to be an alternate route within our judicatory system for dealing with sexual harassment.

But will an "alternate route" suffice? Is it not time for the church to discover how power has been systematically abused to dominate the powerless? Should not the church clearly state that the hierarchical patterns of leadership and ministry which have perpetuated this abuse of power, keeping women and children in a state of fear and insecurity, are sinful? Is the church ready for this?

The church's *reluctance to deal with the issue of human sexuality* also has a bearing on the violence in our societies. This question must also be addressed if we are to be able to fully understand the roots of the violence. All religious traditions have tended to convey warped images of sexuality, providing quasi-divine legitimization for rape and abuse of women's bodies. It is therefore easier to discuss, for example, the economic and political roots of prostitution than the reasons why men seek out prostitutes. The church would rather take a moralistic stand on the women involved than challenge the men to examine their depraved sexuality. The church is quick to oppose abortion even in wartime rather than look compassionately at the future of broken women and of children born out of brutal lust. Pope John Paul II, for example, urged the raped women of Bosnia-Herzegovina to bear their violators' children rather than choose abortion. In a letter to the archbishop of Sarajevo, he wrote that "even in such a tragic situation, [these women] must be helped to distinguish between the act of deplorable violence which they have suffered from men who have lost all reason and conscience, and the reality of these new human beings who have been given life."

It is ironical that women have been simultaneously viewed as child-bearers and evil temptresses. Warped images of sexuality hold women responsible for the advent of evil in the world. The Indian epic *Ramayana* includes a story about the sage Vishwamitra, who is absorbed in penance so intense that it shakes the whole universe, including the heavens and the throne of the lord of lords, Indra himself. Annoyed, Indra sends the beautiful Menaka to earth to dance her way into the soul of the devout sage. Menaka ultimately touches the sage seductively and wakes him out of his trance, enticing him to take her into his arms. The penance is broken, the heavens stop shaking, and Indra recovers his peace.

In Christianity, women have been identified as the source of impurity and death, and their victimization legitimized by attributing the origin of evil and sin to Eve. Through Eve, "man" is said to have lost his immortality, and woman her essential freedom, the evil in the world being epitomized by the pain of childbirth. The dualism in Christianity between male/female, spirit/body, human/non-human and good/evil helps to validate the low status accorded to women. And since "evil" is associated with female, it is a woman's fault if she is raped. It is she who enticed the man to rape her; as popular parlance has it, she "asked for it".

In working with battered women in Minnesota, USA, Joy Bussert reflected on how this aspect of Christian theology has influenced the women's lives:

> Christian theologians like Luther projected "uncontrollable sensuality", and thus responsibility for the fall, onto women as the object of sexuality since sexuality appears to be what they most feared in themselves. Thus [did the theologians] make woman the unfortunate recipient of the Christian adaptation of Platonic alienation (of the soul) from the body, and relegated her to her "rightful" — that is, subordinate — place in relation to man. The higher principles, mind and spirit, were labelled "male" and the lower principles, body and matter, were labelled female. Man represented mind, woman represented body. Man had the capacity for reason and intellect, woman the capacity for emotion and feeling. Man became the rational subject; woman the carnal object. [51]

These theologians fail to consider that in Christ all these odious distinctions were overcome. He tore down the body-soul dualism by accepting women as they were, including their bodies. Some of the moving encounters Jesus had with women spring immediately to mind. We think, for instance, of the unconditional love expressed by the unnamed woman who washed Jesus' feet with oil and wiped them with her hair, or of the faith of the haemorrhaging woman who defied all accepted norms of pollution by touching the hem of his robe, and who received not only healing but acceptance and commendation for her faith.

5. Where Do We Go from Here?

> Christians are called to assist, to be Christ present for those who struggle for their dignity and rights[52]

Is the church present in the pain and suffering of the millions of violated women in this world? The church has been in the vanguard in challenging global economic and political injustice, and articulate in condemning policies and practices that keep millions of people subjugated. As has been rightly said, movements of oppressed peoples for justice and dignity are a spiritual necessity of our times. Then why is the church not a fore-runner in challenging all the forces that hold women ransom to a violent and ruthless world? Why has the theology of the church been virtually silent on this issue? Why has the church in many instances condoned sexual harassment and even violence in its own institutional life? These are the questions women are asking as we call on the church to respond with resolute action.

Solidarity means "being ready to be touched by the other", WCC general secretary Konrad Raiser said recently. What does this mean for the church? Is it ready to immerse itself in the bleeding lives of women, to be touched by our wounded hands? Is the church ready to respond to our vision of a violence-free world, based on our theological and spiritual resources?

Jesus heard women's cries. He not only shared some important insights into the purpose and meaning of his life and ministry with the simple Samaritan woman at the well, but he also acknowledged the context of personal and structural pain in which she was immersed. Jesus gathered the woman's tears and baptized her into a renewed and transformed life. She left her past, symbolized by her water jar, behind her and ran into the town to share with her people the message of salvation she had received.

If we were to gather together the tears already shed and as yet unshed by women around the world, I believe we could baptize the church into a life of solidarity and resolute action.

The women raped in all wars and conflicts, including those who must bear unwanted babies, the women who have been subject to harassment and abuse in pastoral relationships and ecumenical gatherings, the women who have escaped from unsafe homes, the women who have sold their children into prostitution after a life of prostitution themselves — these and many other women call on the church to listen to their cries, but also to support them in their efforts to overcome their pain. They are clear that such solidarity is possible only if the church is ready and willing to support them in their efforts to create a safe space, a secure and free environment, in which they may fearlessly work towards a just and peaceful world for all.

And women say:

Do you wonder that a storm brews
Within a woman who is counted as soft?
Do not be disturbed!
Even now,
Without your solidarity,
We have no intention
Of crossing the storm
Which is our struggle for freedom.
There is a lot of old dirt
Both in your brain and my brain.
Come, let us clean it out and move on.
We should not be fighting each other.
We must be together setting right the wrong in this world.

But before this...
If your legs happen to be on my hands,
Just move them a little bit.

Subhadra
(Translated from the original Tamil)

6. Afterword

During the four years since this book was first published the World Council of Churches has intensified its response to the issue of violence against women. In the context of the Ecumenical Decade of Churches in Solidarity with Women, it has challenged churches to support women in their struggles for a violence-free world and has provided a space for Christian women to voice their theological and ethical responses to the violence they experience. It has also freed women, particularly in contexts where it is most difficult, to speak out boldly about the violence within the life of the church itself. Working with regional and national ecumenical bodies, it has organized a series of consultations on violence against women in each region of the world between 1993 and 1996.

The commitment of women to build networks of solidarity at the regional level, the striking commonality of their analysis and the way in which "life issues" such as this draw women together into a circle demonstrate how women are learning from each other's experience and supporting each other's efforts.

> I stand here unflinching,
> As wave after mighty wave hits at me...
> Rips into my face..., my body,
> Cuts into my heart...
>
> Wave after mighty wave hits at us,
> But we stand here undaunted,
> Unafraid...
> Because we hold each other tenderly
> In the warm circle of feminist power...
>
> This arm encircles the pain of the violence
> he inflicted on you my sister,
> And that one embraces the hurt of a woman marginalized
>   by her colour and her race.
> This arm encircles the woman who is a victim
>   of rape and abuse in a war-torn country,
> And that embraces you my sister who are too old,
>   or too fragile, or too ill.

This arm encircles the woman who is just too lonely,
   too isolated and very alone,
And that embraces my lesbian sister
   who experiences violence at every turn.
This arm encircles the tears of a woman who has lost a son
   – a victim to malnutrition,
And that embraces the wounded feet and hands
   of a girl child who has been sexually abused...

Yes, we hold each other up in a circle of feminist power,
And we stand here unflinching;
We stand here unafraid...
We look into each other's eyes with courage and energy,
A circle of life... of resilient power... and of love.
We hold each other up in a circle of feminist power...
And we dance... and we dance... and we dance...[53]

This circle of resilient feminist power – choosing life, choosing to resist all the death-dealing forces in our world – is emerging as a political alternative in every corner of the world. But as women around the world have discovered, if we are to dance together, to celebrate our sisterhood, we will have to name the violence in our societies. The hidden face of violence has to be exposed, because women know that truth is the first step towards reconciliation and healing.

Women speaking out, unafraid

One of the most significant features of the United Nations' fourth World Conference on Women (Beijing, August-September 1995) was the fact that women spoke out unafraid. The Platform of Action approved at the inter-governmental meeting is strong in its condemnation of the many forms of violence women experience; and it sets out various creative ways in which governments could act. In this connection, the important work of Radhika Coomaraswamy, the UN Special Rapporteur on Violence Against Women, should also be noted. And it would not be an exaggeration to say that the central theme at the fo-

rum for non-governmental organizations (NGOs) along-
side the Beijing conference was violence against women.
Groups from around the world organized workshops on
different aspects of this issue.

One of eight workshops organized by the WCC at this
forum focused on young women demanding a violence-
free world. This workshop was a stage in the WCC programme of building a network of young women in the
ecumenical movement. Its first gathering, in Fiji in
November 1994, had sent a message entitled "I Am
Worthy" to the churches:

> We spoke..., we listened..., we dreamed dreams..., we dared
> to have visions. We brought with us our joys, our hopes, our
> struggles..., from our many churches and nations and our var-
> ied life experiences. We came with a commitment to work for
> a world free from violence. We used our wisdom and our
> creativity to tackle our problems as young women. We came
> to affirm together that we, as young women, are indeed wor-
> thy of full and creative participation in church and society.

Each of the regional consultations on violence against
women made its own declaration or statement strongly
affirming this voice of resistance. All the consultations
identified the various manifestations of violence and
named the unjust structures of power that undergird it.

To African women meeting in Nyeri, Kenya, in May
1994, it was the dominant market paradigm that aggra-
vates the violence:

> In the face of the economic challenges African women, who
> are the primary providers in the households, have struggled to
> find the means for family survival. With the cuts in social
> services, the caring and nursing responsibility rests squarely
> on women's shoulders. Poverty due to the economic crisis is
> a major cause of prostitution. The increased poverty also
> makes women more vulnerable to sexual abuse and harass-
> ment suffered at the hands of those with power, like prospec-
> tive employers.

Elsewhere in the South, and in Eastern and Central Europe, the rapid liberalizing of economies is giving rise to new forms of violence. As Asian women described it in the Bali Declaration (August 1993):

> The myth of "progress" fuelled by its philosophy of "survival of the fittest" is in fact creating more victims, new victims; is creating deeper schisms between the rich and the poor; legitimizing the domination of the powerful over the powerless; carrying us headlong into the vortex of a global market economy destroying and eroding totally our socio-economic systems through international financial institutions that our countries today are totally dependent on and selling out to; a developmental model and an economic structure that is built around a consumer ethic and which has dispossessed the majority of people, desacralized nature, destroyed our cultures and civilizations and denigrated, even denied, the women. The violence of these modern myths has given a new face to the victimhood of women – the feminization of poverty and the further impoverishment of women; the increasing objectification of and commodification of women in newly created industries like sex-trafficking, sex tourism, advertising and pornography.

The Ballycastle Declaration, made by European women meeting at Corrymeela Conference Centre in November-December 1994, reiterated such an analysis:

> The economic order which has achieved dominance in Europe, and which has been exported to so much of the world, imposes conditions of hardship, exploitation and dependency upon many to ensure the comfort and position of others. It assaults our sense of mutual obligation and undermines the individual and corporate quality of life. We are all affected by the structures and systems which institutionalize violence, and are called to understand their roots, so that we may struggle together to overcome their effects.
> The source of violence surely lies in the way we understand and use power. Our religious and philosophical traditions have valued the exercise of power and control as domination of the strong over the weak. We have learned to believe that certain people, embodying certain characteristics,

are more worthy and important than others, and that they have the right to use violence as an expression of that worth. The patriarchal worldview which has shaped our models of family, community, religion and state has deeply ingrained the idea of male supremacy and the right of men to use whatever means they choose to achieve order and control.

The Nyeri Statement urged specific attention to new ways in which women are experiencing violence due to the political context of Africa:

Violence is manifested in the political sphere in the form of legal systems that discriminate against women and have therefore offered them very little justice or protection from gender violence. It is also manifested in the increasing numbers of women and children victims in conflicts. Apart from being terrorized, displaced, raped, assaulted and killed by local fighters, many women have also been victims of rape and sexual abuse by UN peacekeeping forces.

In Latin America, the identification of the violence was detailed and explicit. The women who gathered for a consultation in San Jose, Costa Rica, in September 1993, said:

Sexual abuse includes everything that harms the sexuality of a person, whether or not there has been physical contact. There is both visible and invisible violence that includes eroticism, harassment, incest, rape, spouse rape, unwanted pregnancy, dehumanizing medical assistance in gynaecological consultations and pre- and post-maternity care, childbirth in solitude, loss of employment for pregnancy, the demand of sexual favours by employers, the exploitation of women's bodies for advertising, adolescent maternity, clandestine and unsafe abortions, sexual jokes, sexual illiteracy, indifference of the legal system to sexual crimes, negligent attitude of the authorities when women register complaints, traffic of women, sexual tourism, pornography and prostitution.

For women in the Middle East, speaking of these issues is not easy. Those who met for the regional consultation in Ayia Napa, Cyprus, in June-July 1995 chose to write their Declaration in the first-person singular style, but they speak the same story:

> My voice emerges from a region that has a long history replete with intense struggle and constant wars, and from a society torn by callous religious fundamentalist powers on the one hand and austere modern, imported values on the other hand.

One of the most poetic of the Declarations – "Tofamamao: No More Violence" – came from the women of the Pacific, who met in Apia, Western Samoa, in March 1996. They spoke of what they called the violence "beneath paradise". They wrote:

> Strengthened and encouraged by each other and the unconditional love of God, we reached out to each other and shared our painful experiences and stories of the violence against women throughout our Pacific islands.
>
> We heard of the lack of support by governments, churches and the society as a whole for women in violent situations either at home, in the church or at work or in society. We heard that for thousands of women and girls, home is no longer a safe place, but a place of fear, pain and terror. We wept for the thousands of women who, because of cultural and religious pressures, have suffered violence silently and alone.
>
> We listened to the stories of the violence of poverty, the brunt of which is borne by women; we mourn knowing that this situation is the result of the greed and corruption of our governments.
>
> We acknowledge that the kind of theology taught by the church not only perpetuates violence against women but often condones it. We listened to the stories of the betrayal of women and children's trust by the clergy through acts of sexual harassment and abuse...
>
> We affirmed that we are survivors of the violence and committed ourselves to struggle until justice is done. We listened, we heard, we shared, we struggled, we wept and we prayed...

Culture and religion

Women in all the regional consultations spoke of the quasi-divine legitimation given to the abuse of women and the way in which culture is used systematically to support this as an acceptable fact of life. African women described it this way:

> While recognizing the importance of culture as the basis for affirming our identity, and that there are many positive elements in it, we note that it also has negative, life-denying aspects. Under the guise of culture, gender-based discrimination and practices rooted in the patriarchal tendencies of our cultures and religions, and institutionalized through the church and political systems, dehumanize women as they portray them as property and not as equal partners with men (*The Nyeri Statement*).

The women from the Middle East wrote:

> My oppressors are many: first my vulnerability and ignorance that I have been carrying all along and which I will put off today; second, my society which led me to believe that my body is a curse. I have been the object of abuse and violence as well as of unjust laws, to the extent that I now despise myself. These laws discriminate against me when I falter, while they defend men, with whom I believe I am equal before God. They also muzzle my mouth if I cry. I am searching for a world that hears my silent voice, appreciates me for what I am, encourages and respects my femininity and motherhood genuinely (*The Ayia Napa Declaration*).

Asian women drew attention to the Asian family as a context for control of women:

> The family, along with the state today, has sought to control woman through rigid definitions of sexuality and to appropriate for itself reproductive rights and control over her body; violence and subjugation have been woven into institutionalized forms of religion whose patriarchal tenets have marginalized and domesticated the female and the feminine, shackling her and legitimizing violence against her. Social and legal codes of justice have either been blind to crimes against

women like wife-battering and prostitution that have in fact received tacit social approval; or have seen violations like sexual assault and rape as acts of individual aberration and deviance and have even rendered some totally invisible, as in the case of homophobia (*The Bali Declaration*).

In the Asian consultation there were lesbians present, and they urged the participants to stand in solidarity with them. They described the various forms of violence they experience just because they are lesbians – not only from society, but even from within Asian women's movements. Often this is rooted in a blind denial of sexuality per se. We are not yet able to affirm boldly the right of each individual to make his or her own sexual choices. Forcing individuals to hide their sexual orientation or forcing celibacy on them denies them their human rights. There is also the harsh treatment – sometimes subtle, but often overt – of those who have the courage to "come out" and openly profess their homosexual orientation. The church must provide a word of hope and encouragement to lesbian women, who are too often the target of violence.

The Latin American consultation spoke of how violence maintains cultural inequalities:

> Violence is a historic and cultural construction. It is an instrument for the maintenance of inequalities and is an expression of superiority and strength. The ideological structure is the base that legitimates social relationships of dominance. Especially affected are women, children, the poor, indigenous peoples, blacks and other socially marginalized sectors. The ideological social structure, with its myths that reinforce man's supposed superiority, is used against women, defining their fields of activity and restricting those spheres where women are allowed to participate. These restrictions are taken as if they were natural, justified by philosophy, science and even religion (*The San Jose Declaration*).

European women spoke of "patriarchal dualism" as the heart of the problem:

Patriarchal dualism has deeply affected all the institutions and cultures which have developed in Europe. It has denigrated "the other" in all that differs from, or appears to threaten, the centrality of the powerful white male: women, children, people of different race or colour, those without material substance or wealth, the earth itself. Our political ideologies and systems – from capitalism to communism – have effectively devalued the worth of women in production and reproduction. Personal attack, sexual abuse, nationalistic wars, religious conflicts, racial hatred, economic injustice – these expressions of violence are all based on failures to honour the diversity, respect the worth and share the vulnerability of each person in our common humanity (*The Ballycastle Declaration*).

And the church...?

The regional consultations were equally articulate in naming the violence against women in the church. In a statement on violence against women accompanying the Bali Declaration, Asian women described it in this way:

By paying lip service to the question of partnership between women and men, the church has institutionalized various forms of discrimination. In some forms the violence is physical, but most often it is psychological and emotional violence that is perpetrated by the church. In its most blatant form, violence is experienced in pastoral counselling contexts and in incidents of sexual abuse of women evangelists and social workers in the field. In the Asian context there is a misconception that clergy represent God and therefore in most cases women keep silent and do not protest. Very often the victim is condemned or punished and the man's actions are condoned.

Often, in fact, the church has imposed the concept of partnership as an ideology, ignoring the serious and intentional steps communities must take to reach such a goal. The European consultation heard stories not only of women whose faith, commitment and service the churches take for granted without recognizing it in their decision-making structures, but also of "sexual harassment, misconduct and abuse by clergy and church workers, of women and children wounded by the actions of men who claim the authority of Christ's name – their wholeness fragmented, their anger imprisoned by shame and guilt". Echoing these same sentiments, the Latin American consultation addressed these words to the churches:

> We believe that, as a consequence of the tolerance of these situations, the body of Christ is mutilated. This part that is affected suffers and is marginalized from the possibility of full participation in the community. In tolerating these injustices, the church loses its moral authority and falls into the trap of a double-standard morality. The hope for rebuilding and renewal in Christ is destroyed (*The San Jose Declaration*).

While the North American consultation did not make a statement, the women did point in their report to the theological concepts that have justified violence against women, as well as those which have empowered women who struggle against violence. Although "sin" has long been identified with women's bodies, they observe the cruel irony that sexual harassment and domestic violence are seldom denounced as sins.

The weakness or even absence of this moral authority on the part of the church is also attested in the reports of many of the team visits to WCC member churches which were organized in the context of the Ecumenical Decade. In all, 75 such teams, each composed of two men and two women, visited more than 300 churches and 650 women's groups to reflect with them on how far the churches have come in their commitments made to women at the launching of the Decade. One of the focal issues for all the visits was how the churches are dealing with the issue of violence against women. The team reports give evidence of the total insensitivity of many church leaders to this concern:

Although every church is against violence in principle, our visits unhappily confirmed that not all are totally opposed to its practice. The churches tend to let violent men go free and at the same time prevent women from speaking out against the violence. The subject is seldom if ever mentioned either from the pulpit or elsewhere by church leaders. The failure of the churches publicly to condemn such violence and state clearly that it is against the teachings of Christ appeared with distressing regularity...

In some cases church leaders denied that violence against women is an issue in the lives of church members or clergy; violence was seen as something that happens only in the community outside the church. Mostly however, this is not the case, and too often the perpetrators of the violence against women are members of the clergy and church leaders. In one church we heard clergy say that they would be opposed to violence "except in certain circumstances". One church leader spoke of "disciplining" his wife and being "thanked" by her later. Several others queried the definition of "violence", wanting to distinguish between violence that resulted in death, and "just hitting".

We were also struck by many churches' apparent inability or unwillingness to deal effectively with violence... Those churches who deal with it tend to see violence as an individual problem and concentrate on helping the individual victim to survive.

In many places we discussed theological justifications for the violence against women and misinterpretations of man-woman relations in the Bible. Some men we talked to tried to justify physical violence as a way of helping women to achieve "salvation".[54]

Authority and power

Women theologians around the world are challenging doctrinal and theological assumptions and commonly held categories of theological knowledge which undergird the existence of violence:

We must deconstruct the theo-ethical language and practice that produces, sustains and legitimates violence against women, and we must reconstruct liberating discourses of resistance and well-being. We dare not, however, allow ourselves to be only reactive, but we must allow the work of women against violence to generate new theological categories and visions.[55]

The challenge of this theological reconstruction points women towards a deep "spirituality *of* and *for* life".[56] Searching for such a spirituality, creating and affirming new theological formulations is not easy. Our experience as women shows that creating a safe space for visioning or reimagining can elicit opposition. But it must be done, and we need to stand together in solidarity and in the search for the liberating and protest potential in all religions.

In the regional consultations and team visits it was private conversations with women that were most difficult. Only here could many women speak of their pain – often mingled with feelings of guilt. Some would say, with a trace of disbelief in their voices, "but does the Bible not say that as women we must be submissive?" or, "I *have to* obey my husband; this is what my pastor told me is the behaviour expected of a 'good' woman." To convince women in such situations that there is another truth is not always easy. This dilemma is related to two central concerns of theology: power and authority. In her writings US theologian Letty Russell has explored this theme extensively, noting "everything feminists touch in a patriarchal society seems to turn into a question of authority".[57]

Protestant women theologians in particular have drawn attention to the problematic role played in this context by the authority of scripture and tradition. This is because the starting point for women's theological work in all regions of the world is their day-to-day existential experience of life. How they understand their daily experiences of struggle informs how they will understand the place and authority of the scriptures and other religious traditions. Kwok Pui-Lan rejects the idea of sacralizing the Bible and the canon as a guarantee for truth:

> For a long time such a "mystified" doctrine has taken away the power from women, the poor and the powerless, for it helps to sustain the notion that the "divine presence" is located somewhere else and not in ourselves. Today, we must claim back the power to look at the Bible with our own eyes and to stress that divine immanence is within us, not in something sealed off and handed down from almost 2000 years ago.[58]

Letty Russell writes that "if authority is understood as *authorizing* the inclusion of all persons as partners, and power is understood as *empowerment* for self-actualization together with others, then the entire game of authority shifts."[59]

The issue of authority was raised in an especially sharp way by one of the case-studies undertaken as part of the WCC's Theology of Life programme, which explored contemporary ecumenical social thought through a focus on the ten Affirmations made by the world convocation on Justice, Peace and the Integrity of Creation (JPIC) in Seoul in 1990. A group of researchers in Malawi undertook a study of the affirmation "All exercise of power is accountable to God". As part of the study Isabel Apawo Phiri, a theologian teaching at the University of Malawi, described the struggle of two sets of women.

The first group she wrote about were women from the Blantyre Presbyterian Synod, who decided, after years of fruitless negotiations for better working conditions as church workers and for the right to ordination, to go on a peaceful walk to the synod headquarters to make their demands once again. Their action led to different levels of harassment from the church authorities: the director of the Church Women's Centre was suspended and all programmes of the Centre stopped; one woman was transferred out of her job; some were given early retirement; a Ghanaian was sent back to her own country. All were "severely reprimanded" and told that women cannot take on positions of authority in the churches because "women are sinners".

Phiri's second example grew out of the situation of women at Chancellor College in Malawi. Four female lecturers researched the extent of harassment and even rape of female students in the college by male students and professors. Following the presentation of their findings, the researchers were interviewed on the radio by the Malawi Broadcasting Corporation. This publicity provoked strong reactions from the male students of the college, who were outraged that the truth had been so clearly stated by the women and felt that "their image was tarnished". Isabel Phiri's office and house were stoned and damaged; and students made threats against her life and that of members of her family. Initially, the authorities did nothing to protect the women researchers; then, in order to placate the students, they initiated a Commission of Enquiry to examine the veracity of the findings of the research. Although the Vice-Chancellor upheld the research, it was of no avail. Isabel Phiri was forced to take a leave of absence of up to four years.

If all exercise of power is accountable to God, Isabel Phiri asks, how does one understand this abuse of power by the authorities of the church? If all exercise of power is accountable to God, how can one account for the ease with which a group of male students managed to take control and sabotage and suppress the damning evidence of the rape and abuse of women students?

Ecclesiology and ethics

The fundamental questions raised by the Theology of Life process about how we do theology and understand the church are also taken up in the WCC's recent work on ecclesiology and ethics. Throughout church history there have been efforts to discover the connections between ecclesiology and ethics. The entry point into the debate has varied, but there has always been an underlying awareness that the churches' quest for visible unity and communion is connected inextricably with the authority

by which the church interprets and lives up to its traditions and the way in which we act as Christians in the
world. In fact, it is in servanthood to Christ that the
church discovers its basis; and this is what undergirds its
ethical and moral authority in the world. The WCC's first
consultation on ecclesiology and ethics (Rønde, Denmark,
1993), put it this way: "the church not only *has*, but *is*, a
social ethic, a koinonia ethic".[60] Such an affirmation of
course implies that the churches have the responsibility of
engaging in the moral formation of their community, of
helping to shape their members' character and moral
choices and the actions they take, singly and together. In
doing so, they nurture virtues, values, obligations and
moral visions.[61]

Events of recent years have raised new questions about
this authority of the church because of what many see as
the complicity of churches in the violent political conflicts in the former Yugoslavia, Rwanda and Burundi,
South Africa and Northern Ireland. In each of these situations, a section of the church was itself directly involved
in provoking and participating in the violence, often giving theological legitimation to the conflicts or to the oppression of "the other". This, says Konrad Raiser, has led
to an understanding that

> some of the presuppositions which have been taken for
> granted in the past are beginning to crumble. Regarding the
> church and its self-understanding, the question is no longer
> simply *when and by what authority* the church (as distinct
> from the individual Christian) should take a stance on ethical
> issues. Instead the focus is on what it means to be the church
> in face of the fundamental ethical challenges of our time or,
> to put it differently, how church fellowship can be maintained
> in face of ethical conflicts. It is no longer possible to assume
> the traditional theological bases of the understanding of the
> church as given and concentrate solely on the question of the
> legitimate connection between ecclesiology and ethics. The
> ethical debates surrounding the struggle against racism, the
> relationship of rich and poor and the Christian witness to

peace have opened up a new perception of the reality of the church, which needs to be worked through ecclesiologically.[62]

Unfortunately, women have found it difficult to persuade the churches and the ecumenical movement that the issue of violence against women is as much an issue of ecclesiology as the churches' complicity in political conflicts or internal wars. The experiences of the Decade have demonstrated repeatedly that the veneer of silence with which churches cover over violence against women is a sign of moral failure and that biblical and theological legitimations of this violence call into question the very authority and power of the church as a moral community.

The end of military rule or dictatorship in a number of countries around the world has placed the question of "impunity" on the international agenda: the idea that reconciliation and future harmony in these contexts can be promoted by deciding not to prosecute or punish those who have committed gross human rights violations. In a WCC consultation in Argentina on this critical contemporary ethical question, individual after individual spoke out in shame against their own silence in the face of oppression. Each one admitted that he or she had succumbed to the fear of repression and the possibility of "disappearance". Now they recognized that their silence had in effect sanctioned much of the violence. This meant that many corrupt leaders who had been accused of crimes against humanity could escape without being charged, tried and punished; in effect, "impunity by default – the deliberate lack of action at all".[63]

Suddenly, in the midst of that litany of voices, a woman stood up. She was middle-class and smartly attired. She spoke of the many years of violence she had experienced in her home at the hands of her husband and of her shame at the silence she had decided to maintain. She now recognized her submissiveness as granting impunity to the perpetrator of violence with whom she had lived. Having broken her silence, she would now resist all forms of violence against women. Perhaps her only option is to break away from the abusive and life-threatening relationship in her own home. Does this not challenge the churches and the ecumenical movement to respond to the issue of violence against women as an ecclesiological concern, as serious and as vital as other issues of moral engagement to which the church is challenged?

To continue Raiser's analysis of the new debate, "the radicalizing of these questions becomes especially clear if we take seriously that the scope of ethical responsibility is no longer confined to life in personal relations or in social structures. What is at stake is the preservation of the very foundations of life itself."[64] While he is referring here to our inhumanity to all of creation, can such an enquiry ignore the fact that for women living in unsafe environments life itself *is* constantly threatened? Added to this are the new forms of violence being heaped on women by the colonizing of our wombs through bio-technology and other scientific methodology, controlling women's reproductive choices and capacities – threatening the "very foundations of life itself". Does this not pose important ethical questions to the churches?

In a presentation on ecclesiology and ethics at the WCC central committee meeting in September 1996, African-American theologian Delores Williams made this strong statement:

> Because our world and churches are so afflicted with this atrocious malady of violence against women, we are now called to develop an ecclesiological understanding of ourselves that provides additional marks of the church. Along with the original distinguishing marks of apostolicity, catholicity, unity and holiness, we add "opposition to all forms of violence against humans, nature and the environment". These marks are not only the church's "badge of identity", they also suggest what the mission of the church is supposed to be. The church is to bear witness to the world that it is built upon a tradition of dedicated male and female disciples

supporting each other in the work of hastening the kingdom of God on earth – the kingdom mandated by God to serve all humanity with justice, with care, with peace and with love. There can be neither justice, nor care, nor peace nor love in the church when women are beaten, burned and violated. And when justice, care, peace and love are absent, the church is not the church of Jesus Christ. It is merely an empty house without humanity, without divinity. Lacking justice, care, peace and love, this empty house becomes a domicile where evil can dwell with impunity.

The feminist theological movement begins where women in theology attempt to reconstruct "the question of moral power and authority", but from there it moves to the creative impulses we see around us, as women in faith and faithfulness reconstruct the future image and face of the church as a "community of Christ, bought with a price, where everyone is welcome", as Letty Russell describes it.[65] Her image of the church in the round – of round-table talk and of leadership in the round – is an exciting model of the church inclusive and open, welcoming, hospitable, comforting, prophetic and visibly present in the struggles for justice and life. The ecclesial reality of the church is intricately interwoven with its life as a moral community. It must constantly test its authority to be the moral voice in the world against its ability to respond with courage and conviction to the voices of the excluded, the voices from the margins, the voices of those not yet fully welcomed at the table.

Another recent WCC initiative, the Programme to Overcome Violence has recognized violence in a holistic way. Its Assumptions and Principles state:

Violence originates in part from systems and structures that rob people of the opportunity for humane living conditions... A second system from which violence originates is military rivalry among nation-states... Violence also originates in human hearts and minds. Human sin divides community – people from people, people from God... Families worldwide often employ whipping and beating as a presumed means of discipline – parents against children and husbands against wives. Yet the short-term injuries and the long-term psychological and social damage of such practices, especially as children grow up learning to model the behaviour of their parents, outweigh any presumed benefits gained.

This programme has subsequently taken shape in the Peace to the City campaign, which has selected seven cities around the world, in which both destructive and constructive forces are at work. The campaign will highlight existing creative models of rebuilding community in these seven cities. Among the many forms of urban violence which is rampant in these and other cities, the campaign identifies the concern that

> women dare not venture out at night – or during the day in a wrong part of the city – for fear of violence and rape, only to return home often to find no safety there either. Children, especially those in poor sections, have little safe room to play outside their homes and, like women, too often face the threat of beating and sexual abuse inside their homes.

It is clear that the focus must also be on men. The Decade has stressed that within a well-structured patriarchal society, men have enjoyed some amount of power and have systematically used that power to retain control and inflict violence. Men often claim that they are as much victims of the system as women are. The number of new groups of men in solidarity with women which have come into existence – many in the context of the Decade – is gratifying. These are men who claim their right and responsibility to challenge patriarchal power wherever it exists. They confront issues related to male violence and male sexuality and reflect on how they have benefited from patriarchal institutions – including the theological teachings and practices of the church. This movement has made it clear that there must be intentional programmatic work to encourage men in solidarity with women. Reconciliation will be possible only when women and men are able to look into one another's eyes unafraid.

Looking ahead

The end of the Ecumenical Decade of the Churches in Solidarity with Women in 1998 is in fact only a beginning. The agenda is an unfinished one. The many issues the Decade has brought into the open – the most important being violence against women in church and society – demand continuous attention and responsive action on the part of the churches, the ecumenical movement and particularly the World Council of Churches. WCC General Secretary Konrad Raiser, in his 1994 report to the central committee, lifted up the issue of violence against women: "It is becoming clear that this situation constitutes a fundamental ethical and social challenge that could well be compared to the challenge of racism and its impact on the ecumenical movement in the 1970s."[66] During the central committee meeting of September 1997 he reiterated that "the extent of the violence against women even in Christian communities has come as a shock to many. This poses a challenge to the ecumenical movement which will certainly remain with us... The WCC will be expected to take a lead in responding to this."[67]

The agenda is set. The women of the churches look to the World Council of Churches with eager anticipation. Perhaps the next year will give shape to a constructive and clear programme of solidarity with women on this issue. Perhaps the conclusion of the Decade in 1998 and the 50th anniversary assembly of the WCC in Harare in 1998 – particularly the special hearing on violence against women in the church to be held at the pre-Assembly Decade Festival – will provide the space for the churches and the ecumenical movement and the WCC to respond to the challenge. There can be no rest until there is indeed a world free of violence against women.

Notes

[1] *MATCH News*, Canada, 1990.

[2] The examples that follow are taken from the International Women's Tribune Centre quarterly newsletter *The Tribune*, no. 46, June 1991.

[3] *African Woman*, no. 6, July-October 1992.

[4] Several other studies make the same point; cf. *International Herald Tribune*, 6 November 1991.

[5] Charlotte Bunch, "Women's Rights as Human Rights: Toward a Re-Vision of Human Rights", in *Gender Violence: A Development and Human Rights Issue*, Centre for Women's Global Leadership, Rutgers University, USA, 1991.

[6] These statistics are taken from *The Tribune*, *op. cit.*

[7] "Patriarchy and Violence Against Women", in *Hands to End Violence Against Women*, Women's Inter-Church Council of Canada, Toronto, 1988.

[8] "Sexual Harassment: A Hidden Issue", Project on the Status and Education of Women, USA.

[9] Véronique Ducret, "Harcèlement sexuel sur les lieux de travail", in *Questions au féminin*, February 1992.

[10] Quoted in *Korea Times*, 2 December 1992.

[11] *Madhu Bhushan*, Vimochana, a feminist group in Bangalore, India.

[12] Quoted in *In God's Image*, vol. 10, no. 2, summer 1991.

[13] *African Woman, op. cit.*; the account of the rape is from *Time*, 12 August 1991.

[14] "Rape and Sexual Abuse: Torture and Ill-Treatment of Women in Detention", in *ACT* no. 77, Amnesty International, November 1991.

[15] Catrin Davies in "Free and Equal in Dignity and Rights? The Trafficking of Women to Europe", Quaker Council of European Affairs, Brussels, August 1992.

[16] *Women's World*, no. 24, quoted in "Women Educating to End Violence against Women", Popular Education Research Group, Toronto, Canada, September 1992.

[17] *WARC Update*, World Alliance of Reformed Churches, Geneva, spring 1992.

[18] Foundation for Women, Thailand.

[19] *Exchange and Mart*, 31 October 1991.

[20] The following statistics on Europe are taken from Catrin Davies, *op. cit.*

[21] "God Weeps with Our Pain", in *New Eyes for Reading: Biblical and Theological Reflections from Third World Women*, eds J.S. Pobee and B. Wartenberg-Potter, WCC, Geneva, 1986.

[22] Aruna Gnanadason, poem published in *Indian Express*, no. 3, April 1986.

[23] Rama Joshi and Joanna Riddle, *Daughters of Independence. Gender, Caste and Class in India*, Kali for Women, 1986.

[24] From a conversation between Michael Kaufman and psychotherapist Eimear O'Neill, quoted in *Men's Violence, Women's World*, no. 26, ISIS-WICCE, winter 1991-92.

[25] *CIM Doc.* no. 1, Inter-American Commission of Women, Organization of American States, 1991.

[26] *International Herald Tribune*, 3 July 1991.

[27] From the opening statement by Jan Martensen at a UN Workshop on "Global Strategies for Achieving Gender Fairness in the Courts", Geneva, February 1992.

[28] From "Women in the Frontline" campaign material, Amnesty International, 1990.

[29] "When Christian Solidarity Is Broken", WCC, Geneva, 1992.

[30] *Staff Rules and Regulations*, chap. VI, World Council of Churches.

[31] Musimbi Kanyoro, from the first in a series of lectures at Augustana University College, Alberta, Canada, March 1992.

[32] *Ibid.*

[33] *epd ZA*, no. 130, 10 July 1991.

[34] Quoted by Shirley Jane Endicott in "Theology and Violence against Women", *Women's Concerns*, Canada, winter 1991.

[35] Mercy Oduyoye, Bible study presented at a preparatory meeting for the July 1993 Ecumenical Global Gathering of Youth and Students (EGGYS), Geneva, February 1993.

[36] Fortress Press, Philadelphia, 1984.

[37] Mary John Mananzan, "Who is Jesus Christ?", in *Christologies in Encounter, Voices from the Third World*, vol. XI, no. 2, EATWOT publication, December 1989.

[38] "The National Situation: A Biblical Response from Women", in *Stree Reflect Series*, no. 1, All India Council of Christian Women/ National Council of Churches in India, 1986.

[39] Mercy Oduyoye, "An African Woman's Christ", in *Christologies in Encounter, op. cit.*, emphasis added.

[40] Joanne Carlson Brown and Rebecca Parker, *Christianity, Patriarchy and Abuse: A Feminist Critique*, Pilgrim Press, New York, 1989.

[41] Delores S. Williams, "Black Women's Surrogacy Experience and the Christian Notion of Redemption", in *After Patriarchy: Feminist Transformations in World Religions*, Orbis, Maryknoll, NY, 1992.

[42] Mary Hunt, "Waging War at Home: Christianity and Structural Violence", in *Miriam's Song V*, Priests for Equality, 1992.

[43] Kowk Pui Lan, "God Weeps with Our Pain", *op. cit.*

[44] Nelida Ritchie, "Women and Christology", in *Through Her Eyes: Women's Theology from Latin America*, ed. Elsa Tamez, Orbis, Maryknoll, NY, 1989.

[45] Quoted by Mercy Oduyoye in "Third World Women Doing Theology", *With Passion and Compassion*, ed. Virginia Fabella, Orbis, Maryknoll, NY, 1990.

[46] Marie Fortune, "Family Violence: A Workshop Manual", Centre for the Prevention of Sexual and Domestic Violence, Seattle, USA, 1980.

[47] Mary Hunt in "Waging War...", *op. cit.*

[48] Marie Fortune, *Is Nothing Sacred? When Sex Invades the Pastoral Relationship*, Harper and Row, New York, 1989.

[49] "Ending Violence in Families", United Church of Canada report, 1988.

[50] Marie Fortune, *Is Nothing Sacred?, op. cit.*, 1989.

[51] Joy Bussert, *Battered Women: From a Theology of Suffering to an Ethic of Empowerment*, Lutheran Church in America, 1986.

[52] "When Christian Solidarity is Broken", *op. cit.*

[53] This is an extract from a poem I wrote on the basis of my experiences working with women around the world on the issue of violence. The poem uses the imagery of the folk dance of many Indigenous communities in India, which is done to a simple rhythmic step and a simple melody, usually sung

by a group. Throughout the dance, the women hold each other around the
waist and stay in a semi-circle, never letting go of each other.

[54] *Living Letters: A Report of Visits to the Churches During the Ecumenical
Decade of the Churches in Solidarity with Women*, Geneva, WCC Publications, 1997, pp.26-27.

[55] From the final statement of an international dialogue on "Women Against
Violence", organized in San Jose, Costa Rica, in December 1994 by the
Women's Commission of the Ecumenical Association of Third World Theo-
logians (EATWOT). Women theologians from 24 countries, both North and
South, took part. Cf. *Voices from the Third World*, vol. 18, no. 1, June 1995,
p.216.

[56] *Ibid.*, p.217.

[57] Letty M. Russell, *Household of Freedom: Authority in Feminist Theology*,
Philadelphia, Westminster, 1987, p.59.

[58] Quoted by Chung Hyun-Kyung, *Struggle to Be the Sun Again*, Maryknoll,
NY, Orbis, 1993, p.107.

[59] Russell, *op. cit.*, p.61.

[60] "Costly Unity", para. 6; reprinted in Thomas F. Best and Martin Robra, eds,
*Ecclesiology and Ethics: Ecumenical Ethical Engagement, Moral Formation
and the Nature of the Church*, Geneva, WCC, 1997, p.5.

[61] On the church as a community of moral formation, see "Costly Commitment" (report of the WCC consultation in Tantur, 1994), paras 51ff.; *ibid.*,
pp.39ff.

[62] Konrad Raiser, "Ecumenical Discussion of Ecclesiology and Ethics", *The
Ecumenical Review*, vol. 48, no. 1, Jan. 1996, pp.7-8.

[63] Charles Harper, "From Impunity to Reconciliation", in *Impunity: An Ethical
Perspective*, Geneva, WCC Publications, 1996, p.ix.

[64] Raiser, *loc. cit.*, p.8.

[65] Letty M. Russell, *Church in the Round: Feminist Interpretation of the
Church*, Louisville, Westminister/John Knox, 1993, p.14.

[66] Konrad Raiser, "Report of the General Secretary to the Central Committee,
Johannesburg, January 1994", *The Ecumenical Review*, vol. 46, no. 2, April
1994, p.234.

[67] Konrad Raiser, "Report of the General Secretary to the Central Committee,
Geneva, September 1997", *The Ecumenical Review*, vol. 49, no. 4, October
1997, p.494.

Some Resources

This list of books, articles and church statements is far from exhaustive. There is a great deal of material available in many countries of the world. This is only a sampling of the kinds of resources available. If you would like to consult some of these resources, please do not hesitate to contact us.

Africa

Ilitha Labantu, NY22, Guguletu, Cape Town, South Africa. This black township-based organization provides emotional support, practical advice and education around the problem of violence against women and children.

The Musasa Project, 112 Harare Street, Harare, Zimbabwe. This counselling, public education and research project on violence against women and child sexual abuse publishes a newsletter, *Musasa News.*

Newsletter, Inter-African Committee (IAF) on Traditional Practices Affecting the Health of Women and Children, Ethiopia.

We will make visible the violence done to us, a report on a March 1993 seminar report, National Christian Council of Kenya Women's Desk.

Sexual and domestic violence: help, recovery and action in Zimbabwe, a counselling manual by Jill Taylor & Sheelagh Stewart, Zimbabwe, 1991.

"Violence against women in war", excerpts from *The Liberian manual for training traditional midwives*, Women's Health and Development Program, 1995.

Save the girl-child and restore her God-given rights, Evangelical Presbyterian Church, Ghana, 1996.

Eastern and Central Africa Women in Development Network (ECA-WIDNET) 4th (Oct. 1996) workshop on Violence Against Women, Dar-es-Salaam, Tanzania, *AMECEA Documentation Service*, no.462, December 15, 1996.

Violence Against Women Trainers' Manual, ECA-WIDNET, 1997.

Articles/essays/papers

"Sexual harassment: report from Zimbabwe", in *Echo*, nos. 9-10, 1988.

"Report from Zimbabwe: sexual harassment", in *Sauti Ya Siti*, no.5, March 1989.

"Rape: A crime of violence against women", in *Manela*, vol.1, no.1, Zambia.

"Violence against women in Africa: A human rights issue", in *African Woman*, no.6, Jul.-Oct. 1992.

"Women rise up to fight rape", by Shanta Bryant, in *All Africa Press Service*, Jan. 20, 1992.

"YWCA shelters desperate abused women", by Zarina Geloo, in *Times of Zambia*, Jul. 4, 1994.

"Violence against women in Africa", and "The Nyeri Statement 1994", in *Focus Africa*, March 1995.

"Feminist theology and African culture", by Musimbi Kanyoro, "Violence against women in African oral literature as portrayed in proverbs", by Hazel O. Ayanga, "Hannah, why do you weep?", by Nyambura J. Njoroge, "The status of women in African naming systems", by Mary N. Getui, "Gender violence and exploitation: the widow's dilemma", by Grace Wamue, "Rape as a tool of violence against women", by Margret Gecaga, "A theological reflection on economic violence against women", by Constance R.A. Shisanya, "The Church in Africa and violence against women", by Ruth Muthei James, "Nguiko: a tempering of sexual assault against women", by Hannah W. Kinoti – articles in *Violence Against Women: Reflections by Kenyan Women Theologians*, Grace Wamuea & Mary Getui, eds, 1996.

"Women's shelter in Kenya confronts ancient scourge of wife-beating", by Stephen Buckley, in *International Herald Tribune*, 3 May 1996.

"Rape shadows South Africa: children are victims of nation's collapse into crime", by Lynne Duke, in *International Herald Tribune* Feb. 15-16, 1997.

Asia

"Beyond labour issues: women workers in Asia", Committee for Asian Women (CAW), Hong Kong, 1988.

Violence against women: come together, action pack for campaign on legal reforms, All Women's Action Society, (AWAM), Malaysia.

Working with rape survivors, handbook, Women's Crisis Centre.

Rape in Pakistan, by Shazreh Hussein, Simorgh Collective, Pakistan, 1990.

Pornography, Asian Women's Human Rights Council (AWHRC), Philippines, 1991.

Women and violence: a country report, Centre for Women's Studies, SNDT Women's University, India, 1991.

Breaking barriers: reaching South Asian abused women, a 60-minute video, and *The seven of us survived: wife abuse in the South Asian community*, by Aruna Papp, Multicultural Community Development & Training, Canada.

"Child abuse", an issue of *Verbatim*, Centre for Development and Women's Studies, Madras, India, Jul.-Aug. 1992.

Traffic in women, report of an Asian conference on traffic in women, Seoul, Dec. 1991, Asian Women's Human Rights Council (AWHRC), Philippines, 1993.

"Remembering footsteps in the sands of time": report on the Asian solidarity forum on militarism and sexual slavery, National Council of Churches of Japan, Oct. 21-22, 1993.

Violence against women, creation and humanity, posters and postcards, Asia-Pacific Forum on Women, Law and Development (APWLD), Malaysia, 1993.

"Violence against women", an issue of *Verbatim, op. cit.*, Jan.-Mar. 1994.

Battered women in Malaysia: prevalence, problems and public attitudes, by Rashida Abdullah, Rita Raj-Hashim & Gabriela Schmitt, Women's Aid Organization, Malaysia, 1995.

Report of a consultation on "Spirituality for Life: Women Struggling Against Violence", Jan. 1994, Tagatay City, Philippines, EATWOT (Ecumenical Association of Third World Theologians), Philippines.

The haven becomes hell: a study of domestic violence in Pakistan, by Yasmeen Hassan, WLUML Asia, Pakistan, 1995.

Report of the 4th Asian Women's Solidarity Conference, Manila, in *Update*, LILA-PILIPINA, March 1996.

Articles/essays/papers

"Wifebeating! Not a hopeless case", by Rosella Camte-Bahni, in *Igoroto*, vol.IV, no.4, Philippines, 1990.

"Rape victims do not get decent legal treatment", in *Bankok Post*, Aug. 22, 1990.

"Violence against women in detention: Cherry Mendoza's case", in *Update*, vol.7, no.4, Gabriela, Philippines, Oct.-Dec. 1990.

"A Christian vision of sexual justice: theological and ethical reflections on violence against women", by Lois Gehr, in *In God's Image*, vol.10, no.1, Malaysia, 1991.

"The Gajraula incident" and other articles on rape, by Eunice Britto, in *In God's Image*, vol.10, no.2, Malaysia, 1991.

"Rape: crime against all women", and other articles on violence in *Documentation on women's concerns*, All-India Association for Christian Higher Education, India, April 1991.

"Women fight against sexual discrimination at the workplace", in *Asian Women Workers Newsletter*, vol.10, no.1, Committee for Asian Women (CAW), Hong Kong, March 1991.

"Rape of her privacy", "Break the silence", and "Should the woman be named?", in *WAVES*, AWAM (All Women's Action Society), Malaysia, May 1991.

"Sexual harassment at work: a silenced subject", in *Asian Women Workers Newsletter*, vol.10, no.2, CAW, Hong Kong, June 1991.

"Child brides", in *Observer Magazine*, UK, Jan. 1992.

"Conception of the Cordillera women's crisis center", by Vangie Ram, "Wife abuse: the hidden violence in women's lives", by Cynthia Dacanay, and "Violence against women, issues and perspectives", by Gerry Atkinson, in *Change*, vol.II, no.2, Philippines, May-Jul. 1992.

"International day to end violence against women", in *Change*, vol.III, nos.3 & 4, Philippines, Sep.-Dec. 1992.

"Women's rights, human rights", in *Asia-Pacific Reflections*, APWLD, 1992.

"Fighting against sexual harassment in the workplace", by Hiroko Abe Mizura, in *Asian Women Workers Newsletter*, vol.12, no.4, CAW, Hong Kong, Oct. 1993.

Several articles on sexual violence against women in *Gabriela Women's Update* vol.7, no.5, and vol.8, no.1, Gabriela, Philippines, Dec. 1992 and Jul. 1993.

"Violence targets women", in *Batingaw*, vol.III, no.8, United Church of Christ in the Philippines, Aug. 1993.

"A sub-culture of violence", by Dorothy McRae-McMahon, in *In God's Image*, vol.13, no.2, Malaysia, 1994.

"Update on the proposed domestic violence bill", in *WAVES*, no. 16, All Women's Action Society (AWAM), Malaysia, Mar.-May 1994.

"Filipino brides in Australia: issues of Violence and trafficking", by Chat Garcia-Ramilo & Melba de Guzman-Marginson, in *Asian Migrant Forum*, no.10, Hong Kong, December 1995.

"Woman", by Leena Irene, "An old wives tale", by Sumathy Sivamohan, "Women and violence in Sri Lanka", by Anne Abayasekara, "The ultimate victims of violence", by Manorani Saravanamuttu, "Violence and mind", by Kusuma Devendra,

"What Christianity has to say", by Pauline Hensman, "Meditation on patterns of violence", by Annathaie Abayasekera, Malini Devenanda, Pauline Hensman & Audrey Rebera, "Burdens", by Padma Hensman, "Buddhism, women and violence", by Elizabeth J. Harris, "Creed", by Malini Devananda, "No more tears sister", by Rajani Thiranagama, "Islam and women", by Rehana Mohideen, "Women spirituality", by Annathaie Abayasekera, "Women, law and religion", by Shoramo Tilakawardena, "Wartime", by Shivaramani – articles in a special issue compiled by the Women's Commission, National Council of Churches of Sri Lanka, of *In God's Image*, vol.14, no.4, Malaysia, 1995.

"Some thoughts on violence against women", by Jurgette Nectarina C. Montes, in *Praxis*, no.1, WSCF Asia-Pacific Region, Hong Kong, Jan.-March 1996.

"Sexual harassment: tales of the assembly line", *International Herald Tribune*, May 3, 1996.

"Harassment's deep roots: women's status in Japan feeds the problem", by Andre Pollack, *International Herald Tribune*, May 8, 1996.

"Sexual harassment at Mitsubishi in the US", in *Asian Women Workers Newsletter*, vol.15, no.3, CAW, Hong Kong, July 1996.

"Work global to empower women: NOW speaks on the Mitsubishi sexual harassment case", in *Connect*, vol.1, no.3, IMADR Japan., Aug.-Sep. 1996.

"Violence against women: an international perspective", by Margaret Schuler, "Stopping the violence against women: fifteen years of activism in India", by Govind Kelkar, and "Towards a theory of violence against women", by Ram Ahuja, in *Violence against women*, Centre for Development and Women's Studies, India, 1996.

Caribbean

The Instituto Puertorriqueño de Derechos Civiles (PCICR), Calle Julian Blanco, no.11, Santa Rita, Rio Piedras, Puerto Rico 00925.

The institute supplies information about women's rights, domestic violence and sex discrimination, makes referrals and selects cases Its many resources include a *Manual sobre hostigamiento sexual en el empleo*, 1990, and a newsletter, *Comunica*.

No to sexual violence booklet, ed. Joan French, Sistren Theatre Collective, Jamaica, 1985.

"Notes on rape in the Dominican Republic", by Mely Pappaterra, Santo Domingo, 1988.

Articles/essays/papers

"Day of international solidarity: no more violence against women", in *Comai*, no.XIII, San Juan, Puerto Rico, Nov. 1986.

"Caribbean women organizing", in *Linking women's global struggles to end violence*, Match International Centre, Canada, 1990.

"Child sexual abuse: an issue of male power and control", in *Sistren*, vol.12, nos.2 & 3, Jamaica, 1991.

"Women, violence and the law", by Roberta Clarke, and "Thoughts on domestic violence", by Cathy Shepherd, in *CAFRA News*, vol.5, nos. 3-4, Mar.-Aug. 1991.

"Proposals to reform the rape and incest laws", by Carol Narcisse, in *Sistren*, vol.15, Nos.1 & 2, Jamaica, 1993.

"Violation of women's rights continues in the Caribbean", in *Caribbean Contact*, vol.19, no.10, Barbados, Oct. 1993.

Articles on violence against women in *Quehaceres*, Año 14, Centro de Investigación para la Acción Feminina (CIFAP), Dominican Republic, Nov. 1994.

"El derecho de la mujer a decidir", by Ivonne Wilches, in *Comunica*, Inst. Puertoriqueño de Derechos Civiles, Mar. 1994.

Europe

Church resources

"Violence in marriage", Church of Norway report, includes statements from the 1982 and 1983 bishops' conferences, and information on the church's "Pastoral care for battered women" project.

Decadematerialien on violence against women, Ev. Frauenhilfe in Westfalen e.V., Soest, Germany, Dec. 1992.

Free and equal in dignity and rights? The trafficking of women to Europe, by Catrin Davies, Quaker Council of European Affairs, Aug. 1992.

Safe to grow: guidelines on child protection for the local church and its youth workers, Children's Working Group, Baptist Union of Great Britain, 1994.

Policy on child abuse: policy statement by the House of Bishops of the General Synod of the Church of England and recommendations on its implementation, UK, July 1995.

Decadematerialien on women and child prostitution, Ev. Frauenhilfe in Westfalen e.V., Soest, Germany, Sep. 1996.

Secular resources

Women Against Rape, King's Cross Women's Centre, PO Box 287, London NW6 5QU, UK. This group lobbied successfully to make rape in marriage a crime. Resources include a book, *The power to refuse: rape in the home and outside*, and numerous press releases on this theme.

Viol Secours, C.P. 459, Geneva 24, Switzerland. This group working with rape victims has produced numerous resources on the causes of violence against women and the treatment of victims, including: (1) *Vous avez subi une agression sexuelle. Que faire?*; (2) *Harcèlement sexuel. Que faire?*; (3) *Contre le viol et les violences faites aux femmes. Que faire? Que voulons nous?*, 1988; (4) *Harcèlement sexuel dans le travail. Basta!*, 1990; (5) *Le droit de travailler dans la dignité. Harcèlement sexuel: un abus qui doit disparaître*, 1991; (6) *Viol. Inceste. Violence conjugale. Harcèlement sexuel. A l'usage de celles qui en ont assez de la violence contre les femmes*; (7) *Abus de pouvoir: Les abus sexuels commis par les professionnels de la santé*. 1993.

Sexuelle Belästigung am Arbeitsplatz, Schriftenreihe des Bundesministers für Jugend, Familie, Fraue u. Gesundheit, Bonn, Germany, 1990.

Harcèlement sexuel dans le travail, Swiss Trade Union Federation, 1991.

Halte à la violence contre les femmes dans le couple, Swiss national campaign against violence against women, 1997.

Articles/essays/papers

"L'honneur retrouvé de Maria", in *Femmes suisses*, Jan. 1990.

"Harcèlement: l'impossible combat", in *Femmes suisses*, Jan. 1991.

"EC code proposed to prevent sexual harassment", in *International Herald Tribune*, Jul. 3, 1991.

Report on German ministry for women study on harassment, in *Femina*, Switzerland, Apr. 12, 1991.

"Violences conjugales: un sujet tabou", by Silvia Rapalli, in *Femina*, Switzerland.

92

"Mehr Hilfe bei sexuellen Missbrauch im Pfarrhaus", in *epd ZA*, no.130, Germany, July 10, 1991.

"Wives win right to say no", and "The end to 250 years of sexual slavery", by Flora Hunter & Patrick McGowan, in *Evening Standard*, UK, 23 Oct. 1991.

"Fünf Jahre lang habe ich geschwiegen", in *Tages Anzeiger*, Switzerland, April 16, 1991.

"In the healthy world of the DDR there was no physical violence", in *Die Tageszeitung*, Germany, May 15, 1991. (G)

"In the darkest corners... women enslaved in Europe", by Catrin Davies, in *Around Europe*, no.145, Quaker Council of European Affairs, June 1992.

"Femmes violées, humanité abusée: Femmes et hommes dans l'Eglise", in *Bulletin international*, no.53, France, March 1993.

"Rape in war: the history of the universal soldier", in *Third World Network Features*, no.1089, 1993.

"Women victims of the war in Bosnia-Hercegovina", *ibid*, no.1090, 1993.

"Women in war: a European case", Nato Alerts Nework, Belgium, 1993.

"La violence contre les femmes, l'affaire des hommes", "La violence conjugale fait partie de l'ordre social", by Lucienne Gillioz, and "La violence, un pain quotidien", in *Femmes suisses*, no.2, Feb. 1995.

"A pattern of rape: war crimes in Bosnia", in *Newsweek*, Jan. 11, 1994.

"A matter of power: state control of women's virginity in Turkey", in *Human Rights Watch Women's Rights Project*, vol.6, no.7, from Human Rights Watch, USA, June 1994.

"Violence envers les femmes, atteinte à leur identité", by Marie-Thérèse van Lunen Che, "L'inter-dit ou prise de parole sur un débat clos", by L. Baroni, Y. Bergeron, M. Lagué, "Conférences épiscopales d'Asie: Le rôle de la femme", "Laissez venir les petits enfants", by Margaret Collier-Beudelow, "Culture de guerre, culture de paix", by Claude de Rauglaudre – articles in *Femmes et Hommes en Eglise*, no.67, France, Sep. 1996.

Women and violence, International Anglican Family Network, UK, Lent 1996.

"Unspeakable crimes: child murders stun Europe", and "Nowhere are children safe", in *Time*, vol.148, no.10, Sep. 2, 1996.

Latin America

Servicio de Asistencia a Victimas de Agresión Sexual (SAVIAS),
Alberti 48 (1082), Buenos Aires, Argentina. The service runs training, publications and research programmes and provides practical assistance to women victims.

Boletín, the journal of the Red feminista Latinoamericana y del
Caribe contra la violencia domestica y sexual, ISIS
Internacional, Chile.

La Puerta de las Mujeres, newsletter, Paraguay.

Violencia contra la mujer, Centro National para el Desarrollo de la
Mujer y la Familia (CMF), Ministerio de Cultura, Juventud y
Deportes, Costa Rica, Mar. 1989.

*Quando a vítima é mulher: Análise de julgamentos de crimes de
estrupo, espancamento e homicido*, Conselho Nacional dos
Direitos da Mulher, Sao Paulo, Brazil, 1987, Americas Watch
report, USA, Oct. 1991.

*Violência contra a mulher: Levantamento e Análise de dados sobre
o Rio de Janeiro em contraste com Informações nacionais*, research report, Núcleo de Pesquisa/ISER, Brasil.

Illustrated leaflets on sexual abuse of children, and a booklet for
International Women's Day 1991, Latin American Council of
Churches (CLAI), Ecuador. (S)

Casa de refugio para mujeres y menores, flyer, Ministerio de
Bienestar Social – Centro Ecuatoriano para la Promoción y
Acción de la Mujer (CEPAM).

*Qué dicen los medios de información acerca de la violencia contra
las mujeres?*, Tierra Viva, Guatemala, 1995.

El Asedio Sexual en el Trabajo, Centro de la Mujer Peruano Flora
Tristan, Peru.

"Violencia sexual y normas penales", in *Hoja de datos*, no.2, Red
Feminista Latinoamericana y del Caribe Contra la Violencia
Domestica y Sexual, Chile, Nov. 1993.

*Florecera la esperanza: algunos elementos que se utilizan para
justificar la agresión contra las mujeres*, Universidad Nacional:
Instituto de Estudios de la Mujer/Consejo Latinoamericano de
Iglesias (CLAI), Costa Rica, May 1995.

Articles/essays/papers

"Mulheres e menores vítimas de violencias sexuals", in *Conflitos
de Terra*, Brazil, vol.VI, 1986.

"Dejarse abusar no ayuda", by María Critina Ravazzola, and
"Violencia familar: caminos de prevención", by Soledad

Larraín, in *Ediciones de las Mujeres*, no.14, ISIS Internacional, Italy, Dec. 1990.

"Brazil's male 'honour' loses its legitimacy", in *International Herald Tribune*, Mar. 30, 1991.

"Gaining on sexual violence against women [in Mexico]", in *ListenReaLoud*, vol.11, no.1, USA, 1991.

"La violencia contra la mujer es un delito", and "Testimonio y secuelas del maltrato", in *Puntada con hilo*, Año 1, no.1, Chile, Aug. 1994.

Middle East

Rape Crisis Centre information booklet, Tel Aviv, Israel.

"Facing the law, bruised", by Tina Achcar-Naccache, and "Strategies for identifying and countering domestic violence", by May Majdalani, in *Al-Raida*, vol.XIII, nos.74 & 75, Institute for Women's Studies in the Arab World, Lebanon, 1996.

North America

CANADA

Church resources

Canadian Council of Churches, 40 St Clair Ave East, Suite 201, Toronto, Ont. M4T 1M9 Canada: CCC Policy and protocols regarding sexual harassment.

Anglican Church, 600 Jarvis Street, Toronto, Ont. M4Y 2J6 Canada: (1) "Violence against women",1986 general synod report; (2) "Violence against women. Abuse in society and church and proposals for change", Taskforce report to the 1986 general synod, 1987; (3) Procedures for dealing with cases of sexual harassment, April 1990; (4) Sexual abuse task force policies, Dec. 1990.

Evangelical Lutheran Church in Canada, 1512 St James Street, Winnipeg, Manitoba, R3H 0l2 Canada: (1) Policy statement on sexual harrassment and abuse, 1992; (2) *Broken promises: an educational workshop on wife abuse*, by Inge Kirchhoff, 1987.

Roman Catholic Church, Canadian Council of Catholic Bishops (CCCB), Chancery Office, 355 Church Street, Toronto, ON M5B 1ZB: CCCB statement on violence against women, June 1991.

United Church, 3250 Bloor Street West, Etobicoke, Ont., M8X 2Y4 Canada: (1) Policy statement, principles and assumptions on sexual harassment, approved by the general executive, March 1985; (2) "Sexual harassment is a sin", theological statement 1985; (3) "Sexual harassment in the church", Women in Ministry Committee, Toronto, 1985; (4) *Child abuse*, flyer, 1985; (5) *Women in abusive relationships: the church has been silent too long*, flyer, 1985; (6) *Ending violence in families: a training program for pastoral care workers*, by Roberta Morris, 1988; (7) Procedures for dealing with cases of sexual harassment, Div. Of Ministry, Personnel & Education, April 1990; (8) *Taking Action Against Sexism*, small booklet series, Committee on Sexism, 1994

Church-related resources

"Hands to end violence against women: a resource for congregational use", Women's Inter-Church Council of Canada, 1988.

"And no one shall make them afraid: the church leaders' submission to the Canadian panel on violence against women", Women's Inter-Church Council of Canada, March 27, 1992.

"Bibliographic resources: religion and child sexual abuse", by Shelley Davis Finson, Atlantic School of Theology, 1996.

A message about violence against women, flyer, Inter-Church Working Group, 1995.

Secular resources

How much will the child resemble the mother?, poster, Ontario Medical Association.

"What every man can do to help end men's violence against women", brochure, White Ribbon Campaign, 1994.

Articles/essays/papers

"Violence against women", in memory of 14 young women killed at the University of Montreal, in *Women's Concerns*, United Church of Canada, fall 1990.

"Theology and violence against women", "Flashback", "Take back the night", "I keep the door locked now", "Violence against women – the churches' response", in special issue of *Women's Concerns*, United Church of Canada, winter 1991.

"A violent legacy", in *Vis-à-Vis*, vol.9, no.2, summer 1991.

"Women educating to end violence against women: talking feminist popular education", PERG, September 1992.

"Enlarging the circle: the churches and the search for an end to

96

violence against women", by Vivian Harrower, background paper, Canadian Ecumenical Decade Coordinating Committee, Oct. 1996.

USA

Church resources

National Council of Churches/USA, 475 Riverside Drive, New York, NY 10115-0050, USA: Policy statement on family violence and abuse, Nov. 1990.

American Friends Service Committee, Religious Society of Friends, General Conference, 1216 Arch Street, 2B, Philadelphia PA 19107, USA: Battered women information kit, 1979.

Disciples of Christ, 130 East Washington Street, PO Box 1986, Indianapolis, IN 46206, USA: (1) *The Disciple Woman*, issue on violence against women, 1986; (2) *Working together to prevent sexual and domestic violence* newsletter; (3) Guidelines on sexual contact by pastors and pastoral counsellors in professional relationships.

Episcopal Church, 815 Second Ave., New York, NY 10017-4594, USA: (1) *Sarah*, booklet on sexual abuse of children, Office of Women in Ministry & Mission; (2) *Breaking the silence of violence*, handbook on domestic violence, 1984; (3) *Continuing dialogue*, pastoral study document, House of Bishops, 1991.

Evangelical Lutheran Church in America, 8765 W. Higgins Road, Chicago, IL 60631, USA: (1) *Battered women: from a theology of suffering to an ethic of empowerment*, by Joy M.K. Bussert, 1986; (2) "Sexual misconduct by clergy within pastoral relationships", NW district, 1987; (3) Resolution on sexual harassment adopted by church-wide assembly, 1989; (4) "Sexual abuse and harassment: recommended elements of policy and procedures", Jan. 1991; (5) Sexual abuse and harassment: definitions; (6) *What parishioners can do to understand and prevent clergy sexual abuse*, resource book by Rev. Jan Erickson-Pearson, 1996.

Mennonite Church, 21 South 12th Street, PO Box 500, Akron, PA 17501-0500, USA: (1) *Crossing the boundary: professional sexual abuse*, resource pack, 1991; (2) *Broken boundaries: resources for pastoring people*, and *The purple packet: domestic violence resources for pastoring persons* resource packs, Domestic Violence Taskforce, 1991; (3) *Women's Concerns*, no.112, issue on pastoral and professional conduct, Jan.-Feb. 1994.

Presbyterian Church (USA), 100 Witherspoon Street, Louisville,

KY 40202-1396, USA: (1) Policy statement on sexual harassment in the workplace; (2) Definition of sexual harassment; (3) "Preventing sexual harassment", booklet; (4) "Myths and facts about rape and battery", flyer, Council on Women and the Church; (5) Summary of findings of sexual harassment study, 1982; (6) "Naming the unamed", booklet, 1987; (7) "Violations against the image of God, exploitation of women", flyer; (8) "A time to speak: packet about rape and battery", Council on Women and the Church; (9) "Family violence, a religious issue", study-action guide for congregations, 1988; (10) Policy regarding sexual misconduct by those involved in ministry, adopted by the Rocky Mountains synod, Oct. 27, 1990; (11) Recommended policy and procedures on sexual misconduct for congregations, employers, April 1991; (12) Study paper on family violence, approved by the 203rd general assembly, 1991; (13) "Sexual Misconduct in the church", flyer, Justice for Women Committee, Women's Ministry Unit; (14) *Confronting Violence against women: the church's calling*, a comprehensive resource pack for congregations prepared by the church's Societal Violence Initiative Team. Includes a resource book: *Striking terror no more: the church responds to domestic violence*, curricula, study guides, liturgies and prayer, church policy papers, study reports, resources lists, a set of flyers on domestic violence, clergy misconduct and child abuse, and a Societal Violence Initiative flyer, 1997.

United Methodist Church, 475 Riverside Drive, New York, NY 10115-0050, USA: (1) "Guidelines for eliminating racism, ageism, handicapism and sexism", 1984; (2) Sexual harassment policy for employers, 1989; (3) "Sexual harassment in the United Methodist Church", Nov. 1990; (4) *Ministries with women in crisis*, resource package; (5) "Crisis: Women's experience and the church's response", final report of a UMC crisis survey, 1988-90.

Church-related resources

Center for the Prevention of Sexual and Domestic Violence, 1914 N. 34th Street, Suite 105, Seattle, Washington 98103, USA. The centre focuses on training clergy and lay leaders to deal with the problems. Among its many publications are: (1) *Working together*, a quarterly newsjournal; (2) *Is nothing sacred? When sex invades the pastoral relationship*, by Marie Fortune, Harper & Row, 1989; (3) *Violence in the family – a workshop curriculum for clergy and other helpers*, by Marie M. Fortune, Pilgrim Press, 1991; (4) *Preventing child sexual abuse*, by Kathryn Goering Reid with Marie M. Fortune, Pilgrim Press, 1989; (5) *Keeping the faith: questions and answers for abused women*, video and training resources, 1992.

Laws against sexual and domestic violence: a concise guide for clergy and laity, by Mary S. Winters, J.D., Pilgrim Press, 1988.

Pornography destroys, resource pack, Religious Alliance Against Pornography, 1993.

Secular resources

How to document sexual harassment in the workplace, Working Women's Institute, 1982.

Global context of violence at home and on the job, UN/NGO Liason consultation report, San Francisco, Oct. 25, 1984.

Body psychotherapy with sexual assault survivors, by Eldri Jauch, research project, Santa Barbara, Dec. 1987.

In case of sexual harassment: a guide for women students, Association of American Colleges.

Gender violence, a development and human rights issue, by Charlotte Bunch & Roxanna Carrillo, Centre for Women's Global Leadership, 1991.

All Too Familiar: Sexual Abuse of Women in US State Prisons, Human Rights Watch Women's Rights Project, USA, 1996.

Articles/essays/papers

"Clergy and sexual abuse", by Lindsay Hardin, in *The Witness*, July-Aug. 1990.

"Sex abuse cases rock the clergy", in *Los Angeles Times*, Aug. 3, 1990.

"To greet brothers without fear: the long process of healing after rape", by Judith Floyd, in *Sojourners*, Feb.-Mar. 1991.

"Soul stealing: power relations in pastoral sexual abuse", by Pamela Cooper-White, in *The Christian Century*, Feb. 20, 1991.

"NH church faces up to sexual misconduct", and "Synod delegates to vote on sexual harassment statement", in *United Church News*, Apr. 1991.

"After abuse is liturgy possible?", by Marjorie Procter-Smith, in *Modern Liturgy*, vol.18, no.1.

"Presbyterian bravery under fire", "A bonfire in Baltimore", on Presbyterian report on human sexuality, by Jim Gittings, and "Sex: Justice in church and society", re Presbyterian Church, by

Karen Lebacqz, in *Christianity and Crisis*, May 27, 1991.

"Experts deplore veil of silence over child abuse", and "Youths abused by priests called victims of 'seduction'", by Linda Hossie, and "Ending the stigma and the silence", by Karen Lattea, in *Sojourners*, July 1991.

"Waging war at home: Christianity and structural violence", by Mary Hun, "Like drops of water", by Diane Neu, "Socialization to violence, the wimp factor and a faith response", by Kathleen & James McGinnis, "With clerical abandon", by Catherine P. Grenier, "The tree and its fruit", by Joseph A. Grenier, "Naming, denial and sexual violence", by Carol J. Adams, "The violence against women act: legislation and a legislative strategy", by Sheila K. Mandt – articles in *Miriam's Song*, no.V, Priests for Equality, USA, 1992.

"Finding hope for the victims, the offender and the congregation in cases of clergy sexual abuse or misconduct", by David R. Brubacher, in *Alban Institute*, vol.XVII, no.6, Nov.-Dec. 1991.

"Shattering the myths: rape at church schools", in *Women's Concerns*, no. 108, Mennonite Central Committee, USA May-June 1993.

"A pattern of rape: War crimes in Bosnia", in *Newsweek*, Jan. 11, 1993.

"Domestic violence need not become homicide", in *Just Peace*, vol.4, no.2, Women for Meaningful Summits, USA, summer 1994.

"Societal Violence Initiative Team gets under way in Louisville", by Julian Schipp, in *News Briefs*, PCUSA, Dec. 1995.

"Remembering Jepthah's daughter", by Gwen Sayler, "The big if's", by Linda Johnson Seyenkulo, "Are you hearing bells or alarms", by Karen Titus, "Stories of survivors", by Jane P. Mitcham, "Wheel of fear, wheel of love", by Pamela Cooper-White, "Bread of tears", by Sandra Tjepkema Mintner, "Grief into action", by Mary Latimer Streufert – articles in *Lutheran Women Today*, vol.8, no.10, Nov. 1995.

Pacific

Church Resources

Australian Council of Churches, Private Bag 199, QVB Post Office, Sydney, NSW 1230, Australia: (1) "Breaking the silence: The church and domestic violence", resource pack, 1986; (2) "What does violence against women have to do with Christian

worship?", *Domestic violence resource package*, Commission
on the Status of Women, 1989/90; (3) *Breaking the silence
around domestic violence*, worship resources; *Domestic violence: Handbook for clergy and pastoral workers*, and *Questions
women ask about domestic violence and Christian beliefs*, Joint
Churches Domestic Violence Prevention Programme, Australia,
1995; (4) *Naming violence against women in our church communities: women are speaking out*, booklet (from Victorian Council
of Churches, 1992.)

Anglican Church, PO Box Q190, QVB Post Office, Sydney, NSW
1230, Australia: (1) "Domestic violence", discussion paper,
1989; (2) "Women, the church and domestic/family violence
project", Anglican archdiocese, 1991.

Uniting Church, Commission on Women and Men working to develop sexual harassment guidelines, PO Box A2266, Sydney
South, NSW 2135, Australia: (1) *Responding to family violence:
a kit for discussion, study and action*, Domestic Violence Task
Group, 1987; (2) *Towards wholeness*, brochure, Commission on
Women and Men, 1991; (3) Resolution on sexual violence, UCA
Sixth Assembly, 1991; (4) *Pastoral report to the churches on
sexual violence against women and children of the church community*, 1991; (5) *Sexism – what men can do*, pamphlet, 1991;
(6) *Being faithful to the pastoral relationship*, study guide, including booklets on *Pastoral covenant: professional ethics for
ministers*, *Ministerial ethics – a feminist perspective*, and *Ro-
mantic relationships within the parish*, 1996.

Church-related resources

CASA, the Centre Against Sexual Assault, Royal Women's Hospital, 270 Cardigan Street, Carlton 3053, Victoria, Australia.
CASA set up Project Anna with church funding to provide advocacy for victims of sexual assault within church communities.
Most of CASA's many resources contain extensive bibliogra-
phies and other helpful materials. They include: (1) *Breaking the
silence*, an information pack with brochures on women and rape,
posters and articles, a guide to supporting victims of sexual assault in marriage, and the CASA 1989-90 annual report; (2) An
information pack on sexual harassment, including a guide for
employers; (3) *Stopping sexual assault in marriage: a guide for
women counselors and advocates*, 1990; (4) *Give us water for
the journey*, liturgy celebrated at the WCC Seventh Assembly,
Canberra, 1991; (5) *A pastoral report to churches on sexual violence against women and children of the church community*,

Melbourne, 1991; (6) *Desperately seeking justice*, a resource and training manual on violence against women in a culturally diverse community, 1992; (7) *Sexual assault and other forms of violence within the Australian community: religious and faith perspectives*, papers presented at a national research and training seminar, Nov. 1993; (8) *Public face, private pain: the Anglican report about violence against women and the abuse of power within the church community*, a report on a diocesan domestic violence project, 1994.

Secular resources

The Fiji Women's Crisis Center/Pacific Women's Network Against Violence, PO Box 12882, Suva, Fiji. e-mail: fwcc@pactok.peg.apc.org. The centre runs regular regional training programmes, and produces a great variety of resource materials, including: (1) *Pacific Women Against Violence*, a quarterly regional newsletter; (2) trainers' manuals (e. g.*Counsellor Training Program*, and *Community Education Program*); (3) counselling and community education materials (e. g. booklet series on rape, domestic violence, child sexual abuse, and sexual harassment).

Wife-beating is a crime, pamphlet, Women's Law Committee, Papua-New Guinea.

How to deal with a complaint of sexual harassment, Australian Trade Union Education Authority, 1990.

Through black eyes: a handbook on family violence in Aboriginal and Torres Strait Islander communities, Secretariat of National Aboriginal & Islander Child Care (SNAICC), Australia, 1991.

Videos, policy statement, medical and legal procedures related to violence against women, Fijian women's movement, 1993.

Articles/essays/papers

"Resolving domestic violence: conservative Christians and a social problem", by Rosslyn Reed, in *The Pamphlet Club*, no.361, a supplement to *The Australian Christian*, Churches of Christ in Australia.

"The challenge to the church", *op. cit.*, no.364.

"Violence within the church", *op.* , no.370.

"Bring violence out into the open", in *The Advocate*, RCC, Aug. 23, 1990.

"Sanctity of marriage broken but not her faith", in *Canberra Times*, February 1991.

"Ethics and the minister", in *Australian Ministry*, Feb. 1991.

"Sexual violence in the church", by Marjorie Lewis-Jones, in *National Outlook*, May 1991.

"On forgiving the abuser – Is it possible? Is it necessary?", by Tracy Hansen, in *Priests and People*, vol.5, no.3, March 1991.

"Sexual abuse within the clergy", in *The Age*, July 1991.

"Fact sheets: Violence and its effect in the workplace", and "A woman's story: sexual harassment", in *PAWORNET Newsletter*, Pacific Regional YWCA Office, Fiji, Sep. 1991.

"Women and the law", in *PAWORNET Newsletter*, Dec.8, 1991.

"PNG: violence in paradise", by Ed Morada, in *Reconciliation International*, winter 1992-93.

"Combatting violence against Pacific women: the campaign continues", in *Women's News*, vol.8, nos.1 & 2, Pacific Women's Resource Bureau, New Caledonia, May 1993.

"Thursdays in black", in *A-gender*, Uniting Church, March 1993.

"Sexual abuse complaints procedures approved", in *A-gender*, Uniting Church, autumn 1994.

Articles on clergy abuse in *Crosslink*, June 1997, Aotearoa-New Zealand.

International

Violence against women in the family, UN, New York, 1989.

The Tribune, International Women's Tribune Center newsletter, issue on violence against women, New York, 1991.

Report of the Advisory Group meeting on women, violence and the law, Economic Commission for Latin America & the Caribbean, May 1, 1991.

Women in the frontline: human rights violations against women. Amnesty International, Mar. 1991.

Rape and sexual abuse: torture and ill-treatment of women in detention, Amnesty International, Dec. 1991.

Global strategies for achieving gender fairness in the courts: eliminating violence against women, by Jan Martensen, Under-Secretary General for Human Rights, report to the Human Rights Commission, Geneva, Feb. 5, 1992.

Fact sheet on gender violence, IWTC/UN Development Fund for Women (UNIFEM) Resource Centre, Oct. 1992.

Freedom from violence: women's strategies from around the world, ed. Margaret Schuler, OEF International/UNIFEM, March 1992.

Battered dreams: violence against women as an obstacle to development, by Roxanna Carrillo, UNIFEM), 1992.

Women 2000, no.4, special issue on violence against women, UN

Centre for Social Development & Human Affairs, Austria, 1992.

Second Periodic report on the UN Convention on the Elimination of All Forms of Discrimination Against Women (CEDAW), Finnish Ministry for Foreign Affairs, 1993.

Note on certain aspects of sexual violence against refugee women, Doc. EC/1993/SCP/CRP.2, UNHCR, 1993.

The human body is not a consumer product, brochure, International Abolitionist Federation (IAF).

Women on the move: proceedings of the workshop on human rights abuses against immigrant and refugee women, Vienna, Austria, Family Violence Prevention Fund, June 1993.

Peace: measures to eradicate violence against women in the family and society, report to the 38th session of the UN Commission on the Status of Women, Doc.E/CN.6/1994/4, UNHCR, 1995.

Sexual violence against refugees: guidelines on prevention and response, 1995.

Convención interamericana para prevenir, sancionar y erradicar la violencia contra la mujer, Organization of American States (OAS), June 1994.

Prevention of sexual harassment, extracts from a policy on the prevention of sexual harassment adopted by the executive heads of all UN organizations.

Reports submitted to the annual sessions of the UN Human Rights Commission by the Special Rapporteur on violence against women. All reports in this series are entitled: *Further Promotion and Encouragement of Human Rights and Fundamental Freedoms, Including the Question of the Programme and Methods of Work of the Commission: Alternative Approaches and Ways and Means Within the UN System for Improving the Effective Enjoyment of Human Rights and Fundamental Freedoms: Preliminary Report Submitted by the Special Rapporteur on Violence Against Women, its Causes and Consequences, Ms. Radhika Coomaraswamy, in Accordance with Commission on Human Rights Resolution 1994/85*. These reports are available from the UN Economic and Social Council (ECOSOC). They include the following: (1) Doc. E/CN.4/1995/42, 50th session of the Human Rights Commission, Nov. 22, 1994; (2) Doc. E/CN.4/1996/53, 52nd session, Feb. 1996; (3) Addendum 1: *Report on the mission to the Democratic People's Republic of Korea, the Republic of Korea*. Doc. E/CN.4/1996/53/Add.1; (4) Addendum 2: *A framework for model legislation on domestic violence*. Doc. E/CN.4/1996/53/Add.2; (5) Doc. E/CN.4/1997/47, 53rd session of the Commission, Feb. 1997; (6) Addendum 1: *Report on the mission of the Special Rapporteur to Poland on the issue of traf-ficking and forced prostitution of women (May 24 to June 1, 1996)*. Doc. E/CN.4/1997/47/Add.1.

Articles/essays/papers

"EC code proposed to prevent sexual harassment", in *International Herald Tribune*, July 3, 1991.

"Freeing ourselves from violence", in *Women's World*, no.26, ISIS/WICCE, Switzerland, 1991/92.

"Violence against women", in *Common Concern*, no.77, World YWCA, March 1993.

Human rights: women and violence, UN Backgrounder, Doc. DP/1772/HR-96.00229-Feb. 1996-20M, 1996.

"Violence against women: the hidden health burden", by Lori L. Heiss with Jacqueline Pitanguy & Adrienne Germain, in *World Bank Discussion Papers*, no.255, 1994.

Violence against women and women's human rights, IPPF discussion paper issue 2, International Planned Parenthood Federation, 1995.

"Violence against women: a neglected public health issue in less developed countries", by Lori L. Heise, Alanagh Raikes, Charlotte H. Watts and Antony B. Zwi, in *Social Science Medicine*, vol.39, no.9, 1994.

Several articles on the appointment by the UN Human Rights Commission of a Special Rapporteur on violence against women, in *Libertas* vol.4, no.3, Canada, Aug. 1994.

"UN appoints Special Rapporteur on violence against women", UN press release, April 1994.

"Why are violations of women's human rights different?", "1996 ISIS-WICCE Exchange Programme: Violence against women in situations of armed conflict: an issue of human rights", by Fenella Porter, and "The UN Special Rapporteur on violence against women", in *Women's World*, no.30, ISIS-WICCE, Uganda, 1996.

"The world's violence against women", by Toni Nelson, in *World Watch*, USA, Jul.-Aug. 1996.

World Council of Churches

When Christian solidarity is broken, guidelines for use at ecumenical gatherings, Sep. 1991.

Rape of women in war, report of an ecumenical women's team visit to former Yugoslavia, Dec. 1992.

Living letters: a report of visits to the churches during the Ecumenical Decade – Churches in Solidarity with Women, chap. on violence against women, 1997.

Articles, essays, papers

"Violence against women and sexual harassment", in *Decade Link*, no.8, May 1991.

"Slave trade in Pakistan", "Churches criticized for silence on child violence", and "La violence à l'encontre des femmes", in *Decade Link*, no.11, Aug. 1992.

"Sexual abuse also affects the church", in *Assembly Line*, Canberra, Feb. 1991.

"No longer a secret", by Aruna Gnanadason, in *One World*, Oct. 1991.

"Violence against women: honesty in the church", by Karen Granberg-Michaelson, in *One World*, Nov. 1991.

"Violence against women, church, women and power", by Rebecca Larson, in *One World*, Dec. 1991.

Lutheran World Federation

Articles by women from different regions on violence against women in *Women*, no.32, Jul. 1989.

LWF Council recommendation on violence against women, Norway, June 1993.

LWF Council resolution on violence against women, Geneva, June 1994.

A clear plan of action, section on strategies to combat violence against women in the church, Women in Church & Society, 1993.

"We are witnesses", *LWF Documentation*, no.39, chapter on "Safe places for women and children", March 1996.

Women's holocaust. pg 4 +6   V's
                                   paper
—

p 43 + 45 on sanctity of family
over woman/children's lives
+ safety - come down hard
on this in Bible Study series

• also take on bad sex
for sake of husband's relief
but w/o their own presence. --

425. 673. 0448 Bousons